The World
Designed for
Children

The World Designed for Children

Complete Works of
Hibino Sekkei Youji no Shiro and
KIDS DESIGN LABO

images
Publishing

Contents

188   Chapter 2   Client Speak

OM Nursery, Ibaraki, Japan, Photo by Toshinari Soga / studio BAUHAUS

OM Nursery, Ibaraki, Japan, Photo by Toshinari Soga / studio BAUHAUS

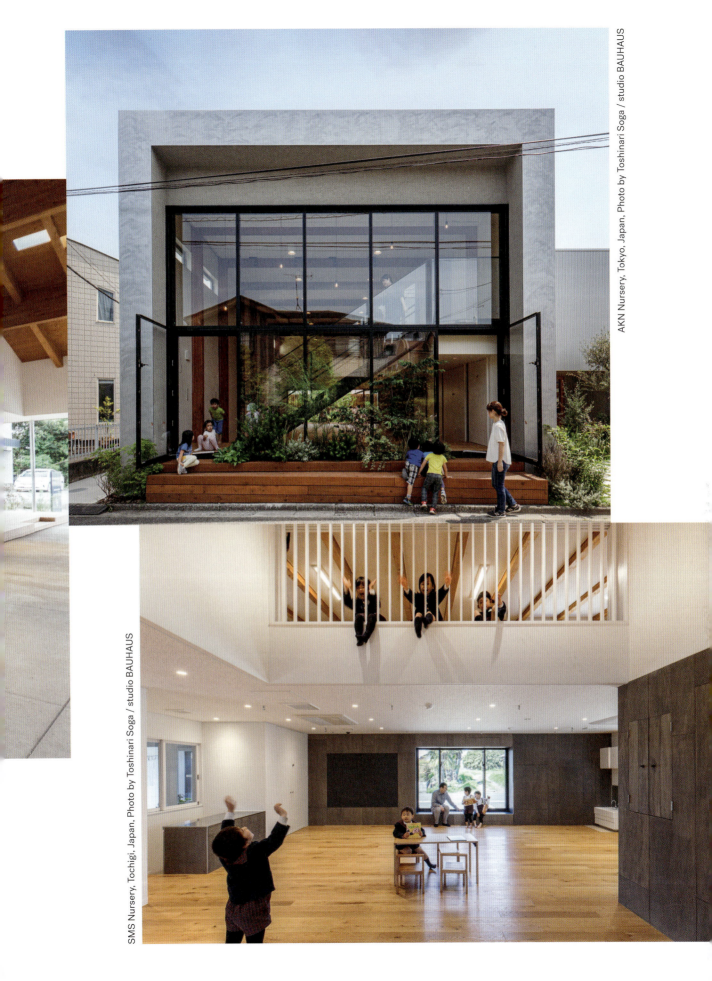

AKN Nursery, Tokyo, Japan, Photo by Toshinari Soga / studio BAUHAUS

SMS Nursery, Tochigi, Japan, Photo by Toshinari Soga / studio BAUHAUS

KN Kindergarten and Nursery, Kagoshima, Japan, Photo by Ryuji Inoue

IRH Child Development Support, Gunma, Japan, Photo by Ryuji Inoue

KN Kindergarten and Nursery, Kagoshima, Japan, Photo by Ryuji Inoue

OM Nursery, Ibaraki, Japan, Photo by Toshinari Soga / studio BAUHAUS

IRH Child Development Support, Gunma, Japan, Photo by Ryuji Inoue

HZ Kindergarten and Nursery, Okinaw, Japan, Photo by Toru Kometani

Introduction

Spaces that Build Your Child's Future

ibino Sekkei Youji no Shiro team has worked on over 560 design projects in Japan as well as overseas; they include kindergartens and nursery schools, primary and secondary schools, and at other spaces where children spend long periods of time.

Hibino Sekkei was established in 1972, when Japan was experiencing stable economic growth, as well as a baby boom. Against this backdrop, the Japanese government prioritized the building of schools and preschools that would be able to accommodate a large number of children, as well as function and operate efficiently. This led to the "harmonica" layout, which became a norm when designing schools all over the country—a rectangular building enclosing a corridor on one side and classrooms on the other. However, since its beginning, Hibino Sekkei has challenged this ordinal way of design and questioned conventional wisdom by trying different and new designs, such as dens under staircases, and wide corridors where children can meet and play. Our design philosophy was solidified and strengthened in 1991 with the establishment of Youji no Shiro, a dedicated team specializing in spaces for children. Youji no Shiro aims to create fun spaces for children, and adults such as teachers and parents who operate within them. Our projects range from construction work to expansion, reconstruction, and renovation.

We believe that spaces for children should be mentally and physically nurturing. To better steer our designs toward these objectives, we conducted firsthand observations of classroom education and childcare setups across the world, where team members visited kindergartens, nursery schools, and educational facilities in thirty countries in a span of three years. We realized that approaches to pedagogy, space, childcare, and educational policies differ considerably across different sociocultural backgrounds. The norm in a country like Japan may seem inconceivable in other countries. Therefore, our designs are grounded in our knowledge of education intentions and the various methods of how children are educated, so that the spaces we create are cultivated from a wide range of perspectives.

Youji no Shiro designs spaces from the child's perspective; they are innovative and encourage spontaneous exercise and creativity. For example, most of our preschool buildings are not closed off by fences or gates, but are instead open to the community.

YM Nursery, Tottori, Japan, Photo by Ryuji Inoue / studio BAUHAUS

We also incorporate playgrounds on different levels, as well as blind spots, stairs, and slopes to encourage physical activity. Restrooms are also, preferably, fitted with large windows to facilitate the use of natural daylight to illuminate spaces.

These are by no means deliberately eccentric design-first features. They are based on deep insights on how our designs affect children—valuable information that has been gathered through collaborations with university laboratories and manufacturers, and which add to the knowledge and experiences we have gained through our creative design work over the years. Our research includes the comparison between the amount of exercise facilitated by the kindergarten buildings pre and post project completion, the effects of different colors on children's psychological states, and the impact of using natural materials and textures, like wood, in classrooms.

Over the decades, Japan has experienced dramatic social changes with its rapidly declining birth rate and increasing aging population. These circumstances have pushed kindergartens and nursery schools into a highly competitive playing field. Children-centric designs must, therefore, incorporate all the fundamental features of an educational facility within a differentiated identity that allows them to stand out. Branding—formed by uniforms, school badges, and the school's logo/crest, among other things—

ST Nursery, Saitama, Japan, Photo by Ryuji Inoue

AM Kindergarten and Nursery, Kagoshima, Japan, Photo by Ryuji Inoue / studio BAUHAUS

must also be aligned with the space, educational policies, and the school's identity.

    This book is a collection of selected prominent works by Hibino Sekkei Youji no Shiro, beginning from the largest, to the smallest in scale. As we share our world, it is our hope that the projects we have put together in these pages help you broaden your understanding of architectural and spatial design for children's spaces, so that you may build bright futures for the children around you.

Chapter

1

Places

for

Children

IZY Kindergarten and Nursery, Aichi, Japan,
Photo by Toshinari Soga / studio BAUHAUS

What
We
Value
in
Children's
Spaces

Architectural design is the core business and starting point for Hibino Sekkei. The Youji no Shiro team within Hibino Sekkei specializes in spatial design for children's spaces and has so far executed 560 design projects, ranging from construction work to expansion, reconstruction, and renovation.

This chapter introduces Youji no Shiro's design approach in recent projects and the concepts we value in our design work; we pride ourselves on originality as Hibino Sekkei strongly believes in producing original and innovative designs and avoids recycling past works.

Site location and size are unique to each preschool and facility, as are educational and management policies. Hence, Youji no Shiro's spatial designs are influenced by the individuality of each project.

This chapter features seven main themes that address specific social and site conditions, among other factors, and within each theme we present wonderfully unique spaces created through repeated dialogs with the management and users of the building.

KM Kindergarten and Nursery, Osaka, Japan, Photo by Ryuji Inoue / studio BAUHAUS

NFB Nursery, Nara, Japan, Photo by Ryuji Inoue / studio BAUHAUS

SUBURBS

Seek Inspiration from the Surroundings

Large suburban sites tend to offer ideal conditions for design, although they often pose unexpected constraints. A common project request is to construct a new building in a vacant area, while an existing building remains in use. While this restricts the shape of the new building, it pushes us to explore best possible alternatives.

Before we begin our design process, we visit the site to understand the owners' requirements, the current conditions, and their vision for the future. We then carefully survey the area around the site. This gives us insight into the unique culture, customs, and history of the area, and these eventually inspire our designs.

For a large site and projects that allow creative liberty, in-depth research and careful listening are critical. Some key aspects to focus on during the preliminary stages are the characteristics of the surrounding environment and the management policies of each kindergarten.

AM Kindergarten
and Nursery

Kagoshima, Japan

COMPLETION: 2015
AREA: 10,129 ft² (941 m²)
PHOTOGRAPHY: Ryuji Inoue / studio BAUHAUS, Toru Kometani

Architizer A+Awards 2017 / 10th Kids Design Award

An all-weather playground
installed underneath the
lifted first floor

^
Dining hall

<
Exterior view

A nursery that boosts exercise levels during play

Located in a port town on the coast of Kyushu's Kagoshima Prefecture in southern Japan, AM Kindergarten and Nursery is set among rich natural beauty and a dense plot of towering trees. While this environment seems like paradise, it is also prone to floods because of its low elevation set 3 meters above sea level. Flooding poses serious evacuation and safety risks to the children in childcare within the kindergarten's premises, especially infants younger than a year old. The crèche, which serves infants to two-year-olds, is elevated and set as a mezzanine between the first and second floors. Following suit, a variety of other spaces at different heights are created, shaping an uncommon interior design.

The crèche on the mezzanine is connected to the dining room in the two-floor atrium at the entrance, and to the loft-style classrooms for children aged three and above. These areas—all at different heights—open up to ten stairways of varying sizes, three slides, climbing poles, and rope nets, creating a free-flowing space with no dead ends. Children get plenty of exercise in the vertical planes, climbing up the stairs and rope nets, and scooting down the slides or coming down the stairs. The "dead spaces" created by these stairs, slides, and other features are reimagined as "secret hideouts" that sometimes also double as libraries, play areas, and creative activity rooms. The piloti—no more

than 2 meters in height—is the distinguishing feature of the center. The children especially love the playground dotted with hills and strung with monkey bars and swings, and the best part: outdoor activities are possible even when it's raining outside.

The site once housed a church and there is still a chapel on the premises. And just like a church, AM Kindergarten and Nursery is open to the entire community, with the lunchroom near the entrance open to local residents; parents can also utilize it as a place to mingle, almost like a community café, when they come to pick up their children from school.

>
Playing den utilizing the space below the staircase

∧
A shallow pool that collects rainwater

‹
A slide installed along the staircase

∨
Library

> A small den, which doubles as hideout for children when needed

∧
The children's restroom has a view of the outdoor garden

∧
Night view

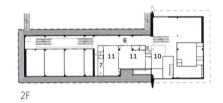

2F

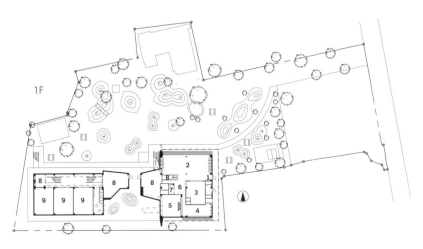

1F

PLAN

1 Entrance
2 Dining room
3 Kitchen
4 Atelier
5 Staff room
6 Corridor
7 Children's restroom
8 Storage
9 Nursery
10 Library
11 Nursery for infants to 2-year-olds

HZ Kindergarten and Nursery

Okinawa, Japan

COMPLETION: 2015
AREA: 11,916 ft² (1,107 m²)
PHOTOGRAPHY: Ryuji Inoue / studio BAUHAUS, Toru Kometani

Architizer A+Awards 2016 / Best Humanistic Care, IAI Design Award 2016 / World Architecture Festival 2016 Finalists / Honorable mention, Kyushu Architecture Prize 2015 / 9th Kids Design Award

Learning from the wisdom of local building traditions

HZ Kindergarten and Nursery is located in Miya-kojima, an island in the south of Okinawa, which is the southernmost Japanese prefecture. Characterized by subtropical oceanic climate, Miyakojima is surrounded by blue ocean and coral reefs, and extends over a Ryukyu limestone foundation.

In addition to having abundant ventilation and shade, the kindergarten also needed to convey a sense of openness; but it was also necessary to seal and secure the center in the event of a typhoon, which is a common occurrence in this hot, humid region. Hence, the design references weather-mitigating strategies that have long been employed in traditional construction practices in Okinawa, particularly in historic Miyako architecture.

The school's outer façade is distinguished by concrete blocks with grid-patterned hollows, a design characteristic of the region. These thick, sturdy structures offer protection from windblown debris and intense sunlight, without obstructing views and ventilation. The color of the exterior tiling approximates red brick, a traditional building material of the region. Traditional floral motifs that are commonly used in local housings are also consciously

< Atelier where children let
loose their creative streaks

∧
Exterior view

incorporated into the design to ensure the
building blends in with the surrounding area.

The building is designed to trace the long,
narrow plot. Visitors who enter from the yard
pass through the facility's studio, followed by
the atrium, courtyard, dining area, and terrace.
Spanning 262 feet (80 meters) in length, the
space makes copious use of wood, forming a
shaded sanctuary swept with cool breezes. The
pleasant breeze and sunlight flood the interior
through the broad entrance facing the yard,
where clusters of banyan and happiness trees—a
species endemic to Miyakojima—allow children to
witness the changing of the seasons as the trees

undergo the different stages of their fruit-bearing
cycle. Sliding windows in the classrooms on the
second floor can be opened to catch the scent of
the ripe fruits, as well as seasonal scents.

The design strives to inspire the children
and staff of HZ Kindergarten and Nursery to
come up with creative ways of utilizing the
facility. At present, the studio, atrium, and dining
area are also used to host events and workshops
conducted by guest speakers. HZ Kindergarten
and Nursery shows the world that a nursery's
potential transcends the scope of early child
education when parents, community members,
and the management work collaboratively.

<
A tunnel-like ground floor, where each child can find a comfortable spot

^
Inner courtyard

Terrace—the thick blocks on the façade gently shade the harsh sunlight of Okinawa

^
Kitchen and dining room

《
A playhouse for younger
children

〈
A maisonette playhouse

⌃
The space at the front
becomes a semi-outdoor
terrace when the sliding
doors are fully opened

PLAN
1 Entrance
2 Staffroom
3 Accessible restroom
4 Playground
5 Terrace
6 Dining room
7 Kitchen
8 Courtyard
9 Atelier
10 Studio
11 Nap room
12 Nursery for infants to
   2-year-olds
13 Nursery
14 Children's restroom

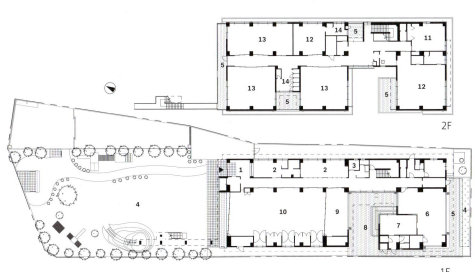

2F

1F

NFB Nursery

Nara, Japan

COMPLETION: 2016
AREA: 12,712 ft² (1,181 m²)
PHOTOGRAPHY: Ryuji Inoue / studio BAUHAUS

Architizer A+Awards 2017 / 11th Kids Design Award

^
Playground with various
"ups" and "downs"

>
Roofed terraces surround the
building

A nursery balanced with an industrial and natural landscape

NFB Nursery in Nara Prefecture, Japan, is located in a city that is older than Kyoto, and which proudly contains numerous World Heritage sites. The nursery school, however, is situated in an industrial area within a lackluster landscape of drab factories. The school had been operating for decades and the building was in need of a renovation.

Instead of detesting the surrounding industrial zone, the design embraces it and makes it a unique environmental factor that inspires the theme.

Similar to factories that are places of creation, nursery schools are spaces for children to create and nurture their dreams and imagination. In gentle appreciation of this similarity, industrial motifs in the interior design, and a muted façade on the exterior reflect the surrounding landscape. These elements are contrasted with abundant greenery in the spacious playground.

Nursery schools are a place of education and personal growth and do well to avoid the use of gaudy colors and excessive play equipment. The school's unique location in an industrial zone, therefore, encourages a creative iteration of a children's space, where they can think and create freely, unfazed by the surrounding gritty landscape.

Borrowing design elements characteristic of a factory also reveals opportunities to learn and discover new things. Pipes in restrooms are left exposed, and transparent ducts are used for ventilation fans, so that children can learn about air flow and water channels in a building. These design elements may appear unorthodox at first, but over time, they become features that generate curiosity among the children.

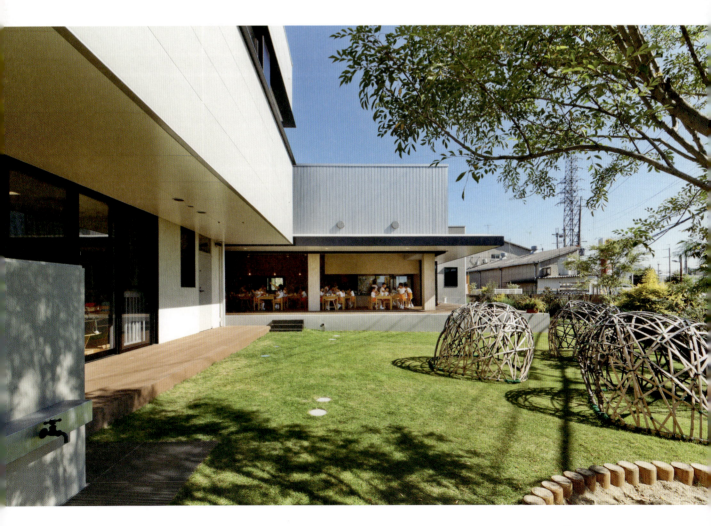

Dining room

^
See-through water pipes that
teach children about water
and energy systems

⌄
View of the corridor

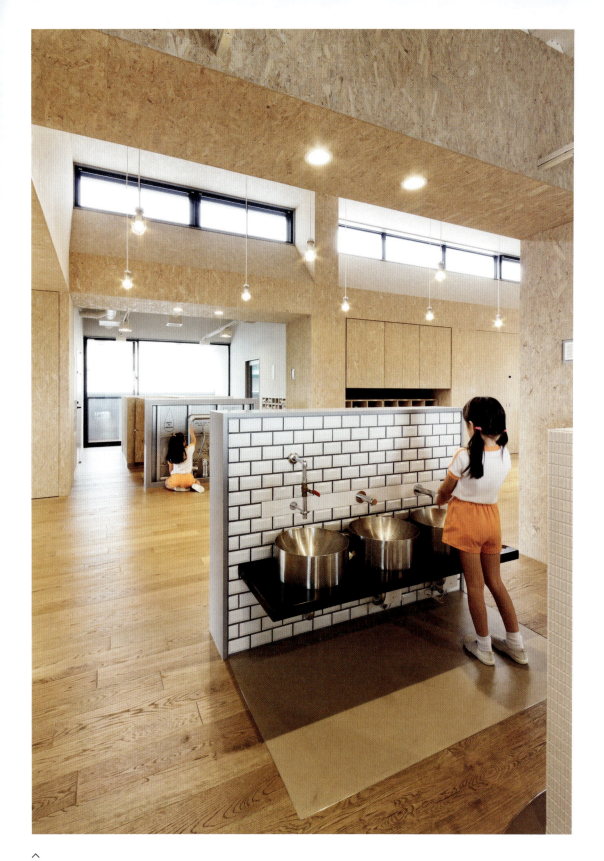

Only natural colors, with
slight accents of stainless
steel are used for the space

∧
A signage made of
galvanized steel sheet

‹
Playful signages

2F

1F

PLAN
1 Entrance
2 Staffroom
3 Kitchen
4 Dining room
5 Terrace
6 Nursery for infants to 2-year-olds
7 Children's restroom
8 Hall
9 Parenting support room
10 Nursery
11 Multipurpose room

IZY Kindergarten and Nursery

Aichi, Japan

COMPLETION: 2020
AREA: 9,332 ft² (867 m²)
PHOTOGRAPHY: Toshinari Soga / studio BAUHAUS

METI Minister's Award 2021 / 15th Kids Design Award /
54th Architectural Award of Central Japan

A traditional yet modern preschool building that blends in with a temple precinct

This preschool is located in Chita Peninsula in the south of Aichi Prefecture, Honshu, Japan, and is a newly constructed preschool that has been built on the abundantly green grounds of an ancient Buddhist temple. The area was once home to highly skilled carpenters who built traditionally designed structures like shrines and temples, and so the design of the preschool respectfully blends with the aesthetic of the temple and its precinct.

Louvers are installed on the temple-side of the preschool to pan a clear exterior, and to also create a gentle connection with visitors to the temple by allowing them to glimpse the activities of the children. The side of the preschool opposite the temple faces open gardens.

Japanese elements seen in traditional temple architecture, such as lattices and patterns in roof tiles, take on contemporary interpretations in IZY Kindergarten and Nursery through natural materials. These elements are incorporated in the walls, partitions, ceilings, and other areas in the preschool as an homage to the surroundings and its rich history, and also to expose the children to such iconic temple features to help them build a recognition of these elements, thereby gradually nurturing a natural fondness within them for the temple and its surroundings.

<

A preschool embedded within a temple

^

The modern architecture stands in sharp contrast with the traditional temple

>

The schoolyard

< A small den, with a sofa beneath

> Children can see through the window into the kitchen

∨ A children-sized hut

∧
Dining room

PLAN
1 Entrance
2 Nursery
3 Hall
4 Stage
5 Indoor terrace
6 Kitchen
7 Children's restroom
8 Nursery for infants to 2-year-olds
9 Office
10 Counseling room
11 Roof terrace

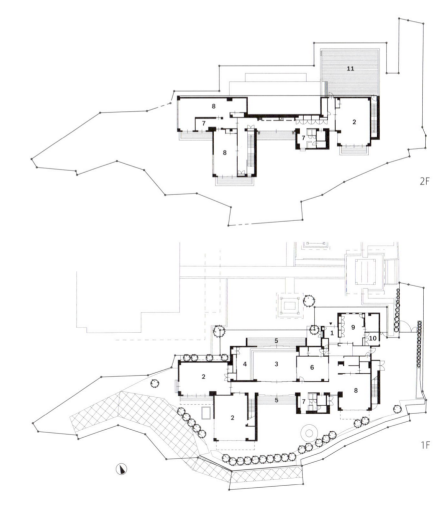

2F

1F

OB Kindergarten and Nursery

Nagasaki, Japan

COMPLETION: 2015
AREA: 15,693 ft² (1,458 m²)
PHOTOGRAPHY: Ryuji Inoue / studio BAUHAUS

Architizer A+Awards 2016 / Best Excellence Award, The IAI Design Award 2016 / Honorable mention, Kyushu Architecture Prize 2015 / Good Design Award 2015 / 9th Kids Design Award

A structure that basks in bountiful nature

OB Kindergarten and Nursery faces a ria coast in Nagasaki Prefecture on the island of Kyushu in southern Japan. Kyushu is abundant in natural resources, with a calm sea extending to the south and beautiful peaks in the north. The site sits on a slope, with a height difference of 39 feet (12 meters) between the mountain and sea. The design of the preschool focuses on creating a structure that imbibes the powerful atmosphere of this natural environment.

The building is designed as a split-level volume that features a slope. Various locations are connected by stairwells, with open areas that allow children to see and hear other people in the building, creating a sense of ease and security no matter where they are. Innovative features that encourage movement are introduced throughout the building and include dens, nets, and blackboard walls. The net connects the rooftop to the lower floor and is particularly popular among the children as they balance and play on it.

∧
An oceanfront building

<
Dining room

>
View from the public road at
the front

The building structure encourages athletic activities across all the floors and highlights narrow crawling spaces that cannot be easily accessed by adults. Also, different types of materials are used as flooring to spur children's curiosities. In this building full of mounds and dips, children grow their physical strength through play. For time alone and introspective moments, the glass-walled atelier provides a conducive space for quiet creative work.

Another important feature of the building is the sea-facing dining room. It has a pleasant environment that showcases the beauty of nature, which parents and guardians can also enjoy when they come by to watch over the children. The open space above creates the impression of a high ceiling, while a deck facing the sea adds to the sense of spaciousness. The structure has become a landmark in the community.

<
Rope structures are installed in various areas of the building for play and fun

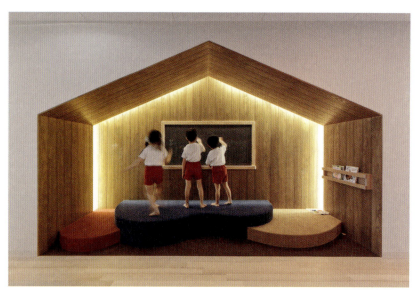

>
Den with sofas and black-board, at a side of the corridor on the ground floor

^
Quiet atelier where children
can concentrate on their
creations

^
Blackboard wall

2F

PLAN
1   Entrance
2   Staffroom
3   Nursery for infants to
    2-year-olds
4   Children's restroom
5   Terrace
6   Atelier
7   Dining room
8   Kitchen
9   Playground
10 Hall
11 Nursery

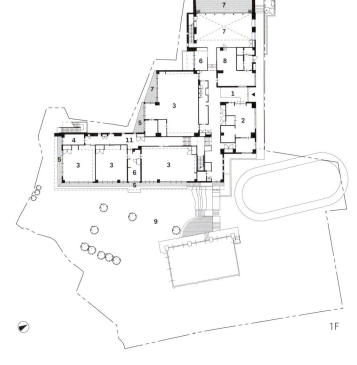

1F

SM Nursery

Tokyo, Japan

COMPLETION: 2015
AREA: 10,527 ft² (978 m²)
PHOTOGRAPHY: Ryuji Inoue / studio BAUHAUS

9th Kids Design Award

View of the inviting grass-covered yard

A nursery with a woodland landscape

This nursery is located in a city in the western part of Tokyo, Japan, and is part of a construction project in a land reallocation zone. The area originally had a lush green cover, which had, unfortunately, gradually disappeared as large-scale construction works progressed. The design of the nursery school considers this loss of nature, while also regarding the preschool as a place where children play, discover, and grow. To that extent, it aims to create a building that supports the local community, as well as reclaim the original landscape and the experiences that were once had with it.

Trees age, iron rusts. To teach children about these laws of nature, a wooden building is designed with reveals of the material composition used. Chemicals have been eliminated from the materials as much as possible, even though that makes them prone to stains; instead, wooden planks with a scent of barley stimulate sensory experiences that complement the architecture.

The playground is planted with numerous fruit trees and herbs, and completed with handmade wooden play equipment. The site has become a countryside treasure trove of discovery and play and it is believed that the space will aptly provide various experiences that will contribute to the children's growth.

<

Instead of stocking the space with ready-made play equipment, the carpenters built an attractive play hut

∨

Children have fun splish-splashing in the shallow waterbody

∧
A blackboard wall by the
entrance also acts as a
communication space where
children can share their
thoughts with their parents

∨
Dining room

∧
Exterior view

<
Alcoves, openings, and steps become different types of spaces for children on various occasions

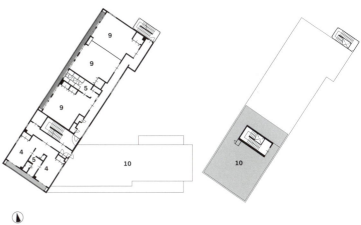

PLAN

1 Entrance
2 Office
3 Counseling room
4 Nursery for infants to 2-year-olds
5 Children's restroom
6 Dining room
7 Kitchen
8 Playground
9 Nursery
10 Rooftop garden

FS Kindergarten and Nursery

Oita, Japan

COMPLETION: 2020
AREA: 7,147 ft² (664 m²)
PHOTOGRAPHY: Toshinari Soga / studio BAUHAUS

15th Kids Design Award

^
Dining room with a full view of the kitchen

⌜
Exterior view

<
A comfortable and all-weather play space is created under the large eaves

A preschool that brings people and nature together

This preschool is located in Northern Kyushu of Oita, Japan, which is a region abundant in greenery. The new building, which replaces the old one, is designed such that children can enjoy the beauty of nature while indoors. The building is covered with a sheet-like roof that resembles a tarp, with trees growing through it. Various natural materials and the colors of trees and foliage are used for the interiors. As the trees provide shade, the sunrays that peek through the branches create glimmering light patterns on surfaces.

With statistics indicating there are fewer children playing outdoors these days, especially in the suburbs, many children are not experiencing the full benefits of an active appreciation of outdoor recreation or interactions socially with the world around them. Accounting for this, the buildings are designed to bring people together and help create connections. One example is the glass-enclosed kitchen that allows children to interact with the staff and also get a glimpse of how their meals are prepared.

^
The atelier space directly
connects to the outside
garden

^
The spacious hall

<
A quiet library corner with a
low ceiling height

∧
Entrance hall

PLAN
1 Entrance
2 Office
3 Kitchen
4 Library
5 Children's restroom
6 Nursery
7 Nursery for infants to
2-year-olds
8 Dining room
9 Counseling room
10 Playground
11 Terrace

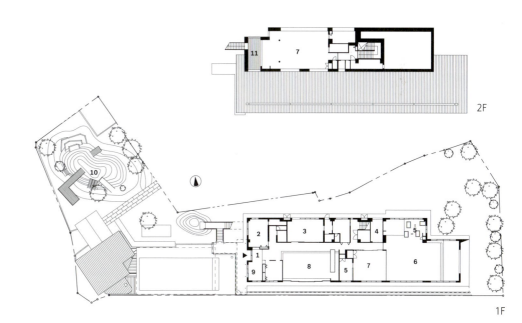

2F

1F

LKC Nursery, Tokyo, Japan, Photo by Toshinari Soga / studio BAUHAUS

Theme 2

View Buildings as Part of the Neighborhood

U rban dwellers tend to prefer closed-off structures due to concerns of crime and safety. However, this may not be the best solution. A better option would be spaces in which children and passers-by can see each other. Such a design also allows the community to watch over the children.

A more tolerable alternative is to create a space within the building that can be frequented by guardians and residents, thus making the preschool a part of the neighborhood. As urban projects generally involve smaller sites surrounded by densely distributed buildings, it is important to first grasp the essence of the urban landscape, and then create designs that reflect preschools as an integral part of the neighborhood.

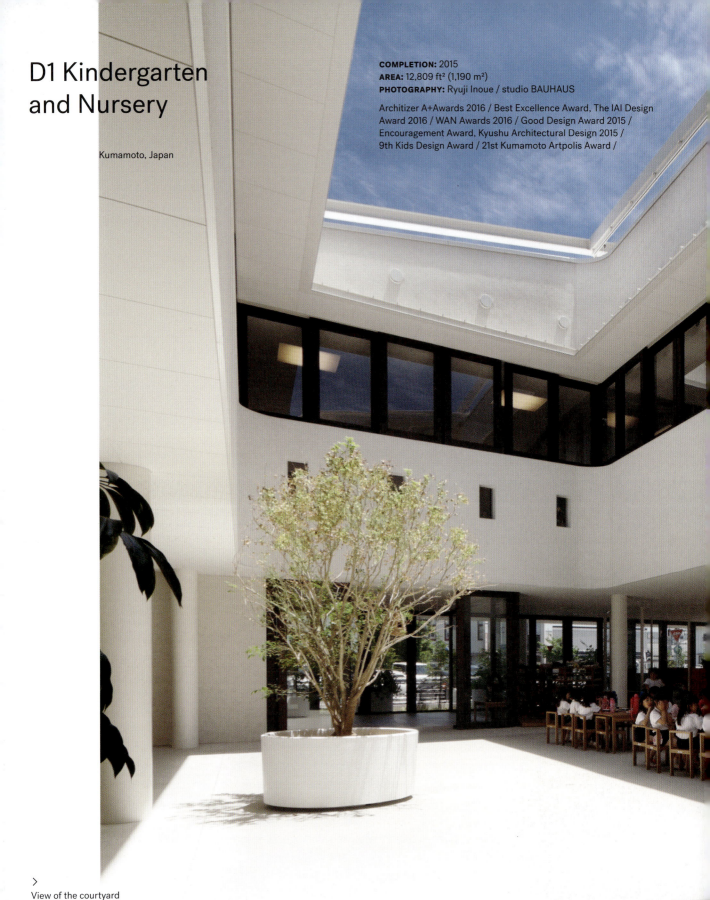

D1 Kindergarten and Nursery

Kumamoto, Japan

COMPLETION: 2015
AREA: 12,809 ft² (1,190 m²)
PHOTOGRAPHY: Ryuji Inoue / studio BAUHAUS

Architizer A+Awards 2016 / Best Excellence Award, The IAI Design Award 2016 / WAN Awards 2016 / Good Design Award 2015 / Encouragement Award, Kyushu Architectural Design 2015 / 9th Kids Design Award / 21st Kumamoto Artpolis Award /

> View of the courtyard

∧
The roof of the courtyard can
be closed when needed

An atrium that evokes the passage of time and seasons

D1 Kindergarten and Nursery is located in Kumamoto, a region in the south of Japan known for its warm climate. The school also operates seven other facilities for early childhood education in the area. To promote globalization, diverse educational programs that include English and ICT education are required in today's early childhood facilities.

To differentiate D1 Kindergarten and Nursery, the concept considers the latest research in neuroscience and psychology to help children become their best selves, giving thought to details such as their daily activities and holistic growth progress. It also considers the best conditions in the human environment, climate, and community to achieve those aspirations. The preschool's design pursues these fundamentals and interprets a creative execution that is tailored for development and enrichment.

The building is shaped like a doughnut and spans two floors. The center on the first floor is connected via the entrance to an outdoor space equipped with a motorized roof that can be left open or closed, creating a range of possible uses as determined by the staff. For example, the roof can be closed to create a sports field or auditorium, which can be used in any weather, or it can be left open on rainy days to allow puddles to form in the courtyard, which is always fun for children to splash and play in. In winter, the children can feel the soft snowflakes and come up with creative games around the falling snow.

A defining feature on the second floor is a spacious, single classroom undivided by partitions or walls. Teachers are free to rearrange the furniture according to the day's

^
After the rain, a shallow pond
appears in the courtyard

lesson plan and classroom activities; they do
not need to close off individual classes with
walls. Teachers who want to hold classes in a
semi-outdoor setting need only open the sliding
windows that line the room, which lead out
to a deck. This design provides both staff and
children a high degree of freedom, emphasizing
independent thought and creativity in early
childhood education.

View of the second floor

∧
A wide terrace runs around
the perimeter of the building

∧
The plan of the wall-less
second floor can be adjusted
by moving chairs and other
small furniture

⟨
Shoe boxes at the entrance

^
Exterior view

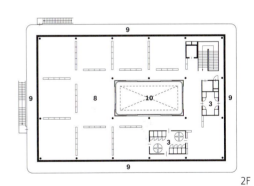

2F

PLAN

1 Entrance
2 Children's restroom
3 Piloti
4 Nursery for infants to 2-year-olds
5 Office
6 Kitchen
7 Courtyard (pond)
8 Nursery
9 Balcony
10 Atrium

1F

AN Kindergarten

Kanagawa, Japan

COMPLETION: 2015
AREA: 14,918 ft² (1,386 m²)
PHOTOGRAPHY: Ryuji Inoue / studio BAUHAUS, Hiromi Asai

Best Institutional and Public Space, Modern Decoration
International Media Award 2016

A nursery that is a hub where the community can interact

AN Kindergarten is located in a residential area in Kanagawa Prefecture, Japan, which serves as a bedroom community for people working in Tokyo. The former building structure was built over forty-five years ago and has been rebuilt to improve seismic resistance, which adheres to stricter standards these days, given the frequent earthquakes in Japan.

The old building had a spacious corridor that was 16 feet (5 meters) wide; adults who attended the kindergarten as children fondly recall it as a place where they frequently interacted with their peers. To preserve the nostalgia and add historical ties to the structure, the corridor is retained in the new building. As a further homage, the center of the building is also designed as a spacious corridor with classrooms, an assembly hall, and other rooms on either side, at the same level. The new corridor is wider than the old one and has a climbing wall, a hut hideout, and a play area under the staircase. One could say that the corridor presents like a spacious forest with hideouts and spots where children can spend time discovering and playing.

Japan has high heat and humidity levels, and next-generation eco-friendly structures that are not completely reliant on electricity are fast gaining popularity. Taking a conscientious step in this direction, a void is designed between the first and second floors and installed with high sidelights to promote natural lighting and cross-ventilation, which reduces the use of air conditioners and artificial lighting during the day.

⌄
A small tunnel underneath the staircase

∧
"Huts" set to float in the atrium are ideal chill-out places for children

＞
A hut hideout

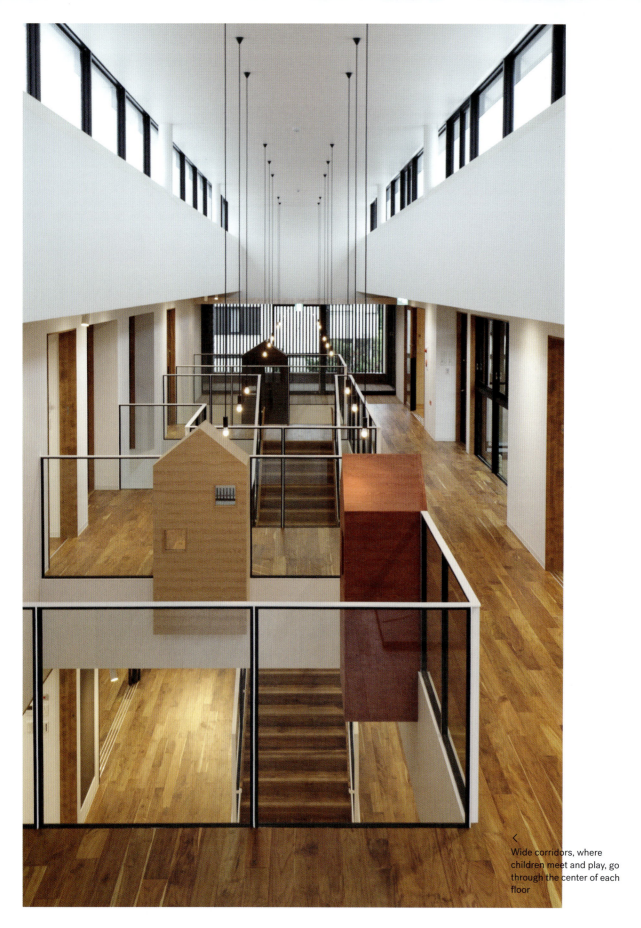

Wide corridors, where children meet and play, go through the center of each floor

∧
Children playing at the
climbing wall and the
blackboard wall

>
Shoe boxes by the entrance

∧
A continuous transition from
indoor to outdoor is created

>
A spacious playground

^
Exterior view from the yard

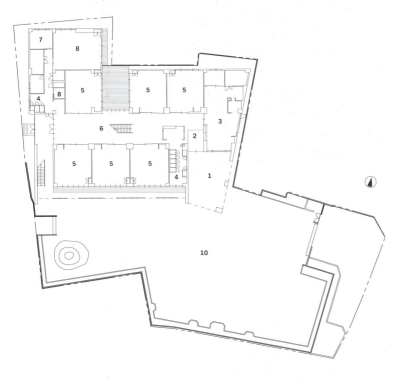

PLAN
1 Piloti
2 Entrance
3 Office
4 Children's restroom
5 Nursery
6 Corridor
7 Parenting support room
8 Meeting room
9 Hall
10 Playground

ATM Nursery

Osaka, Japan

COMPLETION: 2017
AREA: 11,625 ft² (1,080 m²)
PHOTOGRAPHY: Ryuji Inoue / studio BAUHAUS

Architecture Master Prize 2018 / International Design Media Award 2018 / Selected Architectural Designs 2018 by Architectural Institute of Japan / Good Design Award 2017 / 11th Kids Design Award

Recreating classic sceneries of children at play

ATM Nursery is located in a neighborhood that underwent major development in the 1960s as part of Japan's New Town movement, altering the landscape of the neighborhood to one of homogenous multi-unit apartment buildings.

A child's character is often shaped by the nursery the child attends, which is usually crucially influenced by the history and scenery of the land on which it sits. This understanding inspired a design that reinterprets the housing complexes that played such an important role in the town's history, which evoked the feeling of connectedness with others.

The building's outer perimeter is ringed by balconies—another feature of apartment buildings—giving the impression of subtle unevenness. These balconies overlook small hills and land troughs, as well as climbing walls, slopes, benches, monkey bars, and other features of the compound that are incorporated to support the children's physical development as they play. Though children may find it initially daunting, a setting with such rugged and physically demanding elements—when forgiven

^
Each room is opened to the
yard

<
Exterior view

for minor scrapes and challenges—helps instil boldness, independence, perseverance, and a striving spirit in children.

The nursery's interior is designed to draw visitors' gazes to different spots and areas. For example, the kitchen and dining areas have an open layout that allows visitors to see not only the interior and exterior of the building, but also the road beyond. The space is tailored to continuously remind the community of the children's presence by allowing residents little peeks of the activities in the kindergarten, while also giving children glimpses of the bustle outside the compound.

Each classroom has large windows facing the courtyard and a hallway, allowing the children to catch sight of their friends in other classes.

While many nurseries are "closed off" from their surroundings in the interest of security, ATM nursery is deliberately opened-up to allow children to be watched over by the entire community. The nursery is also the epicenter of a vibrant new community culture, as local residents to frequent the terrace to socialize. This also benefits the children's social skills as they get the opportunity to interact with a diverse variety of people.

A building that harmonizes
with the surrounding
landscape

Dining room with a terrace

∧
Local passersby can see the children—this way, the entire community partakes in raising the children

∨
Children can see each other through numerous openings and windows

∧
A two-story hut

∨
Children climbing and
playing on the rooftop

❯
The rope net play area is
designed to symbolize trees,
with leaf litter on the ground

^
View from the front road

2F

PLAN
1 Entrance
2 Office
3 Kitchen
4 Dining room
5 Terrace
6 Parenting support room
7 Children's restroom
8 Nursery for infants to 2-year-olds
9 Playground
10 Nursery
11 Atelier
12 Library
13 Climbing play

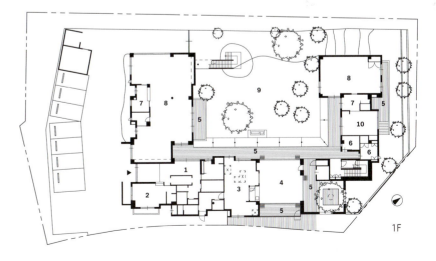

1F

EZ Kindergarten and Nursery

COMPLETION: 2019
AREA: 22,399 ft² (2,081 m²)
PHOTOGRAPHY: Toshinari Soga / studio BAUHAUS

Fukui, Japan

∧
A small cave underneath the staircase

⟩
View of the atrium, where children come up with many imaginative ways to play

A preschool that evokes experiences of the mountains

EZ Kindergarten and Nursery is located in Fukui Prefecture, Japan, which faces the Sea of Japan. The architectural design of the preschool has been inspired by Asuwayama, a mountainous region adjacent to the site, which extends immersive experiences in nature. To create an environment that encourages the children to bring their natural outdoor behavior indoors, their play behavior in a nature setting was first observed. This helped to shape a compound that has a diverse variety of play areas, such as net-based play equipment that allows actions like bouncing and swaying, a shallow pool under the stairs filled with wooden balls, which children can sprawl about in or pick up and throw, and a secret nook with a slope, which they can scale

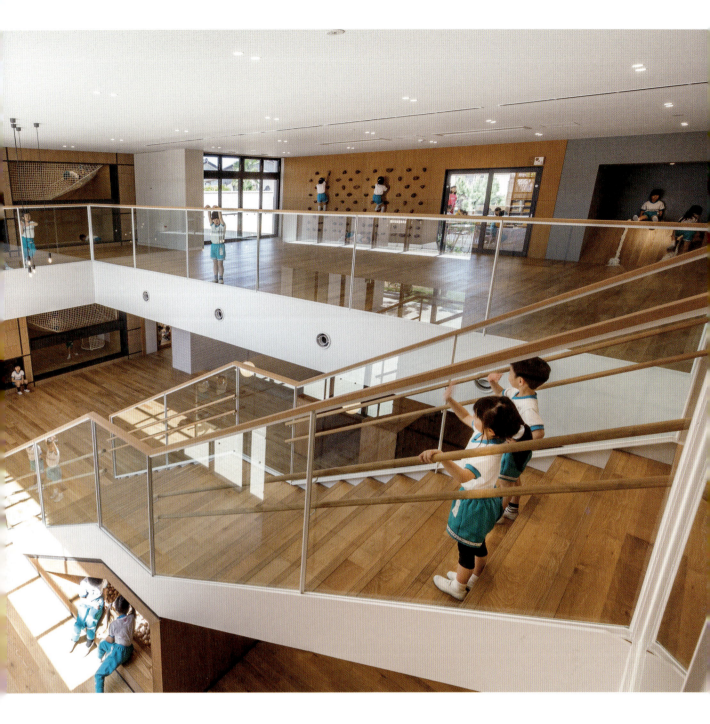

or turn into an impromptu slide; each play area offers the children a host of opportunities to explore their interests and creativity.

To ensure safety, staircases are set along the building wall or enclosed with railings. A staircase is also installed in the center of the nursery to resemble the mountain path that ascends Asuwayama. With multiple levels, it creates various perspectives, making for an interesting play area for the children, allowing them to view the space from a height.

Other similar simply built play areas inspired by nature fill the preschool, so that children can imagine new ways of playing and engage in spontaneous discoveries that bring about a sense of accomplishment.

Dining room

A long wall that encourages children to be creative and active

Hall

⌃
The dining room is open to
the courtyard

2F

3F

PLAN
1 Entrance
2 Office
3 Nursery
4 Children's restroom
5 Terrace
6 Principal's room
7 Kitchen
8 Dining
9 Climbing play
10 Nursery for infants to
2-year-olds
11 Playground
12 Hall
13 Parenting support room

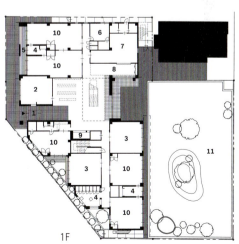

1F

KM Kindergarten
and Nursery

Osaka, Japan

COMPLETION: 2016
AREA: 13,175 ft² (1,224 m²)
PHOTOGRAPHY: Ryuji Inoue / studio BAUHAUS

Architizer A+Awards 2017 / China Good Design Award 2017 /
Architecture MasterPrize 2017 / Good Design Award 2017 / 11th
Kids Design Award

∧
Landscape covered with
greenery

^
A hilly terrain in the courtyard encourages muscle
development

A nursery with active play features despite a limited area

Japan's urban areas have several small-scale day nurseries. Some are set-up in single-room facilities, while many others are built on narrow plots of land. The forty-year-old building housing KM Kindergarten and Nursery, similarly, sits on a small plot. Worn, and with limited floor area, it needed renovating, making the way for a generous redesign that creates a space where children can still get sufficient exercise despite a modest plan.

In the courtyard surrounding the school building, a long slope runs from the ground to the roof; children can run up the slope to the roof, which presents a small play area, and head down the stairs back to the courtyard. This layout allows the children to move freely despite the space constrictions. The use of different levels also increases the scope of physical activity, and the nursery management themselves have since confirmed that the children are more active in the new building than they were in the old one.

Room signage and tapestries also employ textiles and motifs that reflect the region's history as a leading producer of cotton fabrics during the Edo period. As children are exposed to the many varieties of fabrics in the environment, feeling their soft textures, it is hoped that they will naturally develop a love for their hometown.

Dining room

A playing wall and a mirror in the nursery room

Hall—the steps also act as chairs for the children

〈
A quiet atelier space with a low ceiling

〉
Exterior view

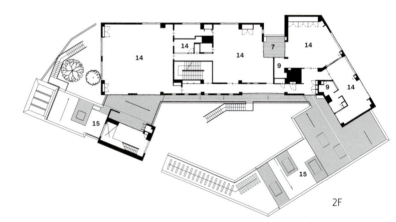

2F

PLAN

1 Entrance
2 Public lounge
3 Hall
4 Kitchen
5 Dining room
6 Library
7 Terrace
8 Nursery
9 Children's restroom
10 Atelier
11 Playground
12 Office
13 Parenting support room
14 Nursery for infants to 2-year-olds
15 Rooftop garden

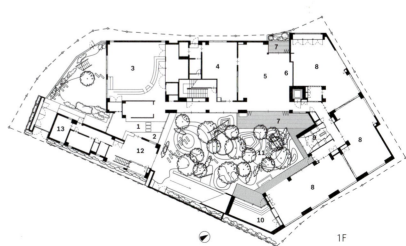

1F

LKC Nursery

Tokyo, Japan

COMPLETION: 2018
AREA: 3,702 ft² (344 m²)
PHOTOGRAPHY: Toshinari Soga / studio BAUHAUS

12th Kids Design Award

A nursery where the community can interact

LKC Nursery is located in one of the most prestigious residential areas in Tokyo, Japan. While the townscape is old-fashioned, the area features high-rise residential towers, commercial and cultural facilities, and other recently constructed amenities. These features have attracted many young affluent households into the area. To counter the increased urbanization, the nursery overlooks a large river, and is envisioned as a space where the children can experience changing seasons and human connections. The school has also been imagined as a neighborhood hub where the community, nature, and art can interact.

∧
Entrance hall that features a
gallery-like interior

＞
A small path in the garden

＜
Existing trees on the site
were preserved as much as
possible

The architecture is linear and evokes a
modern feel. To complement the culturally
conscious community—with some residents
even visiting cultural centers in Shibuya and
Aoyama—artistic translations have been
incorporated as architectural elements—for
example, reflective panes that have been used
in the façade to mirror seasonal changes and
the movement of people around. An atelier is
also included in the layout to encourage artistic
creations and pursuits; there is also a gallery
that exhibits artworks. These elements stimulate
the children's sensitivity to art and allows them
to interact with people and each other through
nature and art.

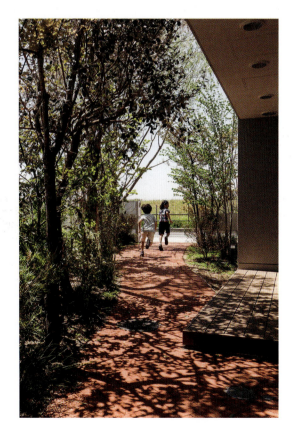

∧
The art gallery with a good
view of the river at front

∨
The atelier has a homey feel
and opens to the garden

∧
Children can see their meals being cooked through the window

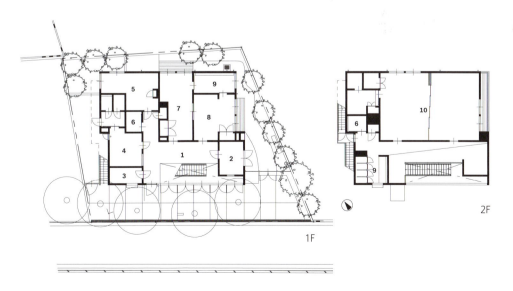

PLAN
1 Entrance hall
2 Atelier
3 Office
4 Kitchen
5 Staffroom
6 Accessible restroom
7 Nursery for 2-year-old children
8 Nursery for 1-year-old children
9 Children's restroom
10 Nursery

1F

2F

M, N Nursery, Kanagawa, Japan, Photo by Toshinari Soga / studio BAUHAUS

Theme 3

INTERIOR PROJECTS

Bring Nature Indoors

An increasing number of preschools are being built inside residential buildings and commercial complexes these days. In these situations, façade design, utility piping, and wiring are determined by the original building design.

These preschools' designs usually prioritize bringing nature indoors. Trees are planted on terraces, and a multitude of ways to introduce greenery into the space are eagerly explored. In these designs, windows are crucial as they allow for natural lighting and cross-ventilation. Materials like earth and wood extend and maintain the children's relationship with nature, so that their development is holistic and well-rounded.

CLC Beijing

Beijing, China

COMPLETION: 2017
AREA: 4,650 ft² (432 m²)
PHOTOGRAPHY: Hibino Sekkei

Architizer A+Awards 2019 /
Best Environment Friendly Award, The IAI Design Award 2018

**A flexible modular system
that can be adapted to the curriculum**

This was a design project for a members-only childcare support center located in central Beijing (China) on a development site lined with high-rise apartment complexes. Intended for young households on the block and in the neighborhood, this facility is open to not only children, but also their parents and local residents, thereby functioning like a community hub.

The remodeling aimed to transform the space from an original design that was considered unsuitable for a nursery and kindergarten. Inspired by Beijing's *hutong*, which are narrow streets that pervade the city's older districts, an "alleyway play" design concept is created. Small structures were built within an original half oval-shaped space with a high ceiling to create different types of "alleys."

This design can be easily replicated and rearranged in a different location/venue to fit the needs of that particular local community and education program.

The center is designed as a combination of container-sized modules with a loft-like space in the upper section. Each module houses a single program and users can freely dismantle and reorganize the walls of the module according to the children's learning needs and curriculum.

The corridors formed by the spatial layout of these modules resemble alleyways, and along these alleyways spaces for children to gather or read have been created.

The design's color palette features only two colors—one for the modules' outer walls and the other for the floor, walls, and ceiling—creating a simple yet warm ambiance. This modular design keeps procurement and maintenance costs low while conferring every new center a unique "signature" style.

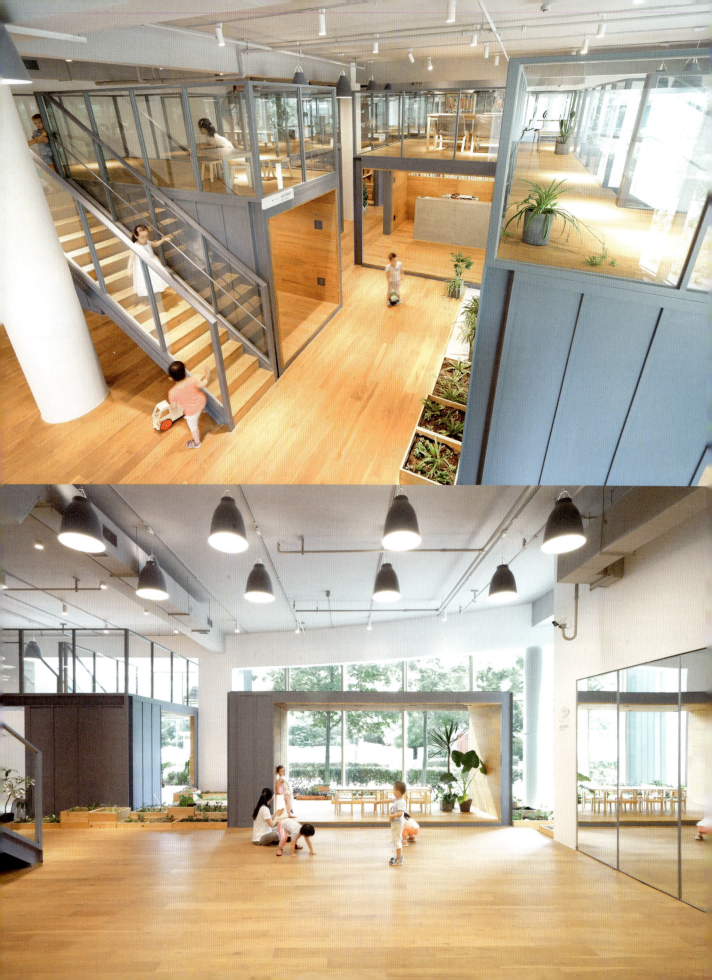

Alleys of different widths and heights are created around the container modules

Container-sized modules are built within the space

Children playing in the hall

Library nook beneath a module

∧
A child trying to climb up the
floating module

>
Library

Inside a module

>

Night view

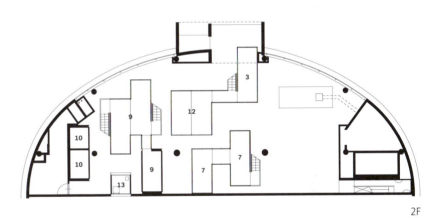

2F

PLAN
1   Entrance
2   Lounge
3   Community garden
4   Dining room
5   Den
6   Playroom
7   Multipurpose study room
8   Reception
9   Library
10 Children's restroom
11 Nursery for infants to
    2-year-olds
12 Café
13 Toy library

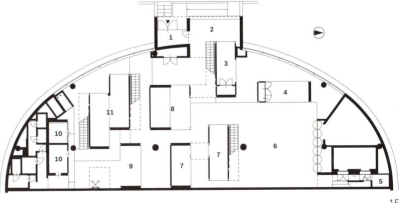

1F

M,N Nursery

Kanagawa, Japan

COMPLETION: 2017
AREA: 4,219 ft² (392 m²)
PHOTOGRAPHY: Toshinari Soga / studio BAUHAUS

< View of the hall

An urban space designed for both kids and grown-ups

The location of the site is a seaside urban area in central Yokohama, Japan, milling with visitors who come to indulge in shopping and leisure, as well as people working in the area's high-rise buildings. M, N Nursery is a corporation-managed nursery located in one such high-rise building. Established by the company—a wedding organizer—for its employees who work weekdays and holidays, the nursery is open year-round.

In the interior planning, a low wall facing the streets, that folds and bends along two sides of the nursery, plays an important role. Holes in the wall connect the indoors with the outside, and parts of the wall morph into benches and tables. Such variations to the wall's form create numerous places that encourage children to play freely. An area for parents has also been included and designed with special attention to create an environment suitable for grown-ups. This space features more contemporary furniture, such as monotone tables, which complement the modern and urban landscape outside.

The nursery features a dual design focus: nurture children's creativity and serve as an intermediate space for parents as they transition between their "home" and "work" mental states. To that extent, the interior and furniture are comfortable and the atmosphere is thoughtfully muted to lead relaxation and offer a brief respite as parents wait to pick up their children.

> The nursery is on the second floor of the building

⌄
A drawing window that is visible to the public

∧
The folding wall creates
various interesting nooks

>
Children enjoying the city
view

<
Dining room with a kitchen
counter

PLAN
1 Entrance hall
2 Nursery
3 Children's restroom
4 Office
5 Kitchen

KB Primary and Secondary School, Nagasaki, Japan, Photo by Toshinari Soga / studio BAUHAUS

Theme 4

RENOVATION

Renovate with Social Evolution in Mind

Japan's high economic growth during the 1970s coincided with a baby boom, which was followed by an accelerated demand for kindergartens and nurseries. Today, more than four decades later, many of these preschool buildings have reached the end of their serviceable life.

As a general construction guideline, buildings in Japan must be built to adapt to changes in seismic safety standards, as well as social conditions. Often, the preferred type of adaptation is renovation and expansion rather than rebuilding. Our designs are based not only on the objectives of meeting various standards, renewing facilities, and improving functional aspects, but also on a strong awareness of the school's vision. Considering Japan's declining birth rate, it is essential that our designed spaces have a degree of malleability, so that they can adapt to changing needs and objectives that may arise in the future.

ATM Kindergarten and Nursery

Shizuoka, Japan

COMPLETION: 2019
AREA:
Building for children—66,198 ft² (6,150 m²)
Building for infants—8,525 ft² (792 m²)
PHOTOGRAPHY: Toshinari Soga / studio BAUHAUS

14th Kids Design Award

A space where children and locals of all ages can interact

ATM Kindergarten and Nursery is located near Tokyo, Japan, in a seaside town famous for its hot springs, and attracts many visitors from the city on the weekends. The area thrives on tourism and many of the younger generation living there are migrating to cities, causing a decline in the overall population and a rise in the elderly population. The preschool is part of a municipal project that aims to revitalize the neighborhoods in the town by improving childcare facilities in the area, as well as the quality of living.

Renovation works spanned the municipal elementary school and a nearby nursery school—structures that are more than fifty years old—to create a kindergarten and a nursery. The original layout in the old buildings presented rows of dull, uniform classrooms; this was reconfigured to create a space that allows seamless communication between the kindergarten and nursery school students, as well as between parents and children. To that extent, walls were torn down to allow a natural flow that enables ease of movement. The nursery has also been opened to the community by removing the external enclosing fence. In the front of the building is a space where locals of all ages can interact, making it a more welcoming environment for children and parents alike.

<
Kids' kitchen and dining room: sunlight and cool breezes are drawn into the basement via the atrium

∨
Beyond the nursery are the atrium and kids' kitchen

∧
Entrance hall

∨
Children's paths of move-
ment and sightlines meet
randomly in the building

∧
A corridor without walls extends through the nurseries, allowing children and parents to communicate freely with each other

⟩
Net play and a horizontal ladder

Playroom

Curious children can sit at
the counter and look into
the kitchen

Dining room

〈
Dining room terrace next to a
pond

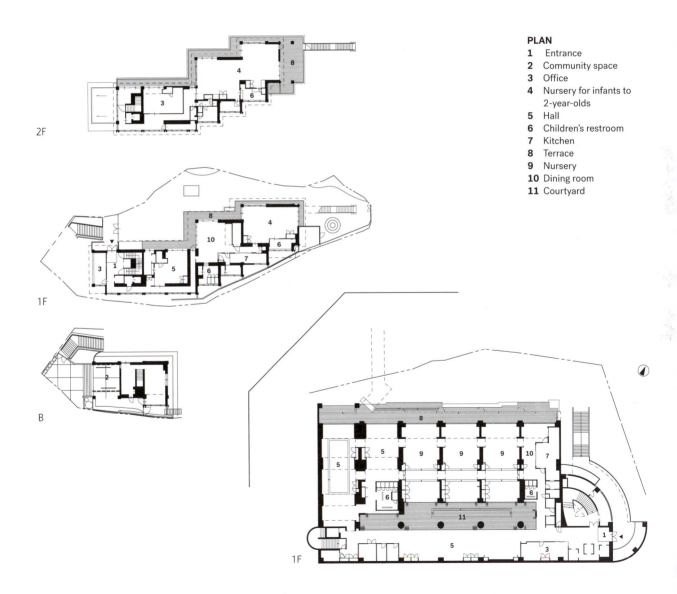

PLAN
1   Entrance
2   Community space
3   Office
4   Nursery for infants to
    2-year-olds
5   Hall
6   Children's restroom
7   Kitchen
8   Terrace
9   Nursery
10 Dining room
11 Courtyard

2F

1F

B

1F

KB Primary and
Secondary School

Nagasaki, Japan

COMPLETION: 2019
AREA: 63,033 ft² (5,856 m²)
PHOTOGRAPHY: Toshinari Soga / studio BAUHAUS

Popular Choice Winner, Architizer A+Awards 2020 /
Good Design Award 2019

Tea ceremony room

A primary and secondary school recreated from a closed-down structure

A closed-down secondary school in a port town in Nagasaki Prefecture, Japan, was renovated into an integrated primary and secondary school. The existing secondary school was a sturdy structure made of reinforced concrete. To accommodate a lean budget, the building frame has been retained, with renovation works extending mostly to the interiors and furniture, to create a thoughtfully planned design that is equipped to fulfil modern educational approaches such as ICT education and active learning.

A key feature of the school is the furniture, which reflects the function of each room. Trapezoid desks in the art room can be rearranged into different layouts depending on the activity and the number of students, and in the learning room, comma-shaped desks and chairs on castors facilitate creative activities conducted for groups of various sizes. Every item of furniture is intended to promote lively and self-directed activities.

Wood and other natural materials expose children to the change in the appearances of these materials over time, in turn helping them learn about, and in turn understand the value of natural materials. The school uniforms have also been designed in collaboration with local designers to complement and enrich the overall design theme of the school.

This project is particularly important to Youji no Shiro as it explores holistic design that extends beyond architecture and furniture. Even though major architectural changes were not introduced, a conventional school has been successfully transformed into one with abundant opportunities for learning and discovery.

Exterior view—the building behind is also a part of the renovated school

∧
Dining room surrounded by wood

＞
Home economics room

IT classroom

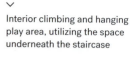
Interior climbing and hanging play area, utilizing the space underneath the staircase

Atelier—all the furniture in bespoke pieces designed by KIDS DESIGN LABO for this project

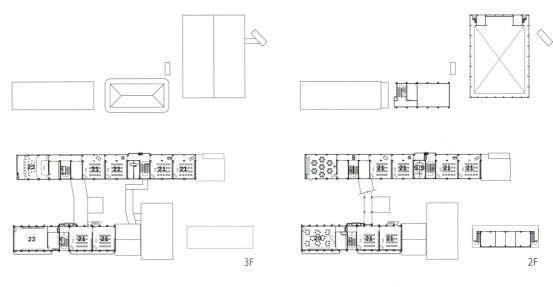

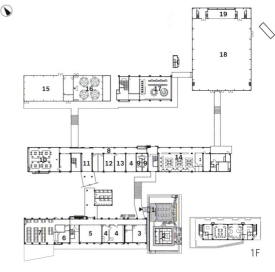

Library

3F

2F

1F

PLAN

1 Entrance
2 Tea ceremony room
3 School nurse's office
4 Meeting room
5 Multipurpose room
6 Kitchen
7 Dining room
8 Corridor
9 Restroom
10 Home economics room
11 Exhibition space
12 Office
13 Principal's office
14 Teacher's room
15 Factory
16 Atelier
17 Library
18 Arena
19 Stage
20 Science classroom
21 Classroom
22 Multipurpose room
23 Music room

MK-S Nursery

Kanagawa, Japan

COMPLETION: 2017
AREA: 1,711 ft² (159 m²)
PHOTOGRAPHY: Kenjiro Yoshimi / studio BAUHAUS

Finalist, Architizer A+Awards 2018 / 12th Kids Design Award

A base created from a residential building with an attached shop

MK-S Nursery is located in a residential district in Japan's Yokohama, a city close to Tokyo. MK-S Kindergarten, the parent institution, sought a facility that would be able to serve as a preschool and an after-school childcare center for its students, and opted to renovate the building across the street and appropriately transform it into a suitable center equipped to the task.

The original structure was a forty-year-old wooden house with a shop on the first floor and a residence on the second floor. To fulfil the requirements for a preschool and an after-school childcare, two adjacent buildings were partially reinforced and repaired to form a facility with four classrooms. As the facility is a subsidiary of the kindergarten across the street, its design theme follows the kindergarten's design concept, "Satellite," to create a relation through appearance. This allows the facility to draw out

<
Exterior view

a background link to the kindergarten, but also define itself apart from it, and be more like a base independent of the kindergarten.

The buildings' existing exterior walls have been retained under a new perforated façade to reflect a galaxy. The sense of depth created lends a new image to the old building. House-shaped windows on the street-facing side catch attention and spark interest in the preschool among passers-by as they glimpse the lively movements of the children within. The sense of depth lends a new image to the old building. The look and feel of the interior is aligned with the exterior through a similar contemporary yet warm décor. A floor-to-ceiling multifunctional unit in each room integrates classroom equipment, such as monitors and desks, and also cleverly incorporates shelves designed as teaching tools. Timber as the main interior material creates a natural aesthetic that is cozy and comforting as it is comfortable, completing the interior with an inviting and friendly ambiance.

Classrooms—the floor-to-
ceiling unit stores classroom
equipment as well as
children's toys and learning
tools

<
Children in English class

∧
House-shaped windows accent both the interior and exterior of the building's design

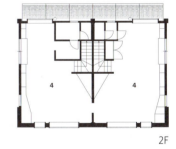

2F

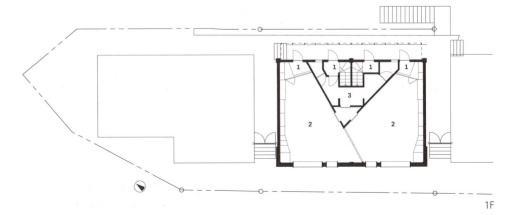

PLAN
1 Entrance
2 Nursery
3 Children's restroom
4 After-school care room

1F

QKK Nursery

Kanagawa, Japan

COMPLETION: 2016
AREA: 1,614 ft² (150 m²)
PHOTOGRAPHY: Ryuji Inoue / studio BAUHAUS

10th Kids Design Award

A nursery school with a garden that stimulates children's senses

The building of this nursery was originally a standalone Italian restaurant that was converted—together with its attached garden— into a licensed nursery for thirty-four infants. To work within a modest budget, changes to the exterior were limited, and priority was directed toward areas that needed refurbishing.

Part of that included maintaining the original interior partitions and unifying them using wood and steel. Play spaces, named "Houses," are incorporated throughout the school to nurture children's development by encouraging the use of all their senses when playing. For example, the Artist House has a blackboard floor that children can freely draw on; the Music House has a floor that emits sound when stepped on or pressed; and The Good Smell House is filled with the fragrance of dried flower bouquets and wood.

As interacting with nature has been known to help nurture a child's mental and emotional stability, the exterior courtyard has been transformed into a small garden with a vegetable patch and flowering plants. This connects the children to a richly green environment that calms their senses while it helps teach them about gardening, nature, plant/animal life cycles, and even the food they eat, instilling an appreciation of the nature around them.

^
Numerous plants and
vegetables that thrive in the
garden

<
View of the garden

^
Dining room

>
Classroom

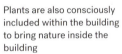
Plants are also consciously included within the building to bring nature inside the building

^
Unique house-shaped playing areas

PLAN
1 Entrance
2 Office
3 Kitchen
4 Accessible restroom
5 Nursery
6 Children's restroom
7 Terrace
8 Playground

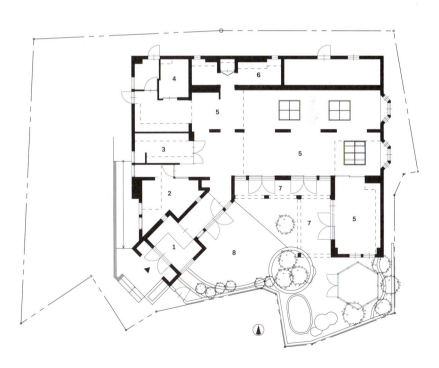

KNO Nursery, Nagasaki, Japan, Photo by Toshinari Soga / studio BAUHAUS

Theme 5

WOODEN STRUCTURE

Explore Wood Interiors that Give Children a Sense of Warmth

Since our early years, Hibino Sekkei has embraced the use of wood in preschool buildings, as well as in interiors, as wooden surfaces provide psychological benefits that bring out positive behavioral traits. For a more in-depth analysis, we conducted a study on the impact of wooden interiors on children, in collaboration with a small panel made up of specialists in Japan from a variety of fields. They include Masato Nishimoto, a lecturer at the Faculty of Engineering, Graduate School of Engineering, University of Fukui; Shinsuke Kawai, an associate professor at the Graduate School of Life and Environmental Sciences, Kyoto Prefectural University; and Shoji Imai, a professor at the Graduate School of Engineering, Mie University. The results of this research were submitted to the Architectural Institute of Japan in 2019.

We found that wooden interiors in preschools have a calming effect on children due to their natural properties, and in turn improve their concentration levels. Unlike spaces made with artificial material, wooden interiors also expand learning and discovery by creating a comfortable environment that fosters self-assurance, self-awareness, trust, and interaction. These qualities are nurtured through simple actions like sitting down on the floor, huddled together, or lying down to color, focusing on their task at hand. When children feel physically comfortable and safe, they learn better, and are also more confident. The simple action of sitting on the floor, encouraged by a warm and inviting environment, extends this level of comfort.

Sitting close to such wooden surfaces also allows them to discover the character of the material as they can observe the grain patterns and wood knots. This creates opportunities for experiential learning that reaches beyond the boundaries of books.

SMW Nursery

Kanagawa, Japan

COMPLETION: 2018
AREA: 8,848 ft² (822 m²)
PHOTOGRAPHY: Toshinari Soga / studio BAUHAUS, Kosuke Tamura

Best Excellence Award, IAI Design Award 2018 / 12th Kids Design Award / 4th Japan Wood Design Award

∧
View from the courtyard—the single-story building adopts well to the surrounding residential area

＞
Each classroom leads out to an inviting outdoor terrace

∧
A pond that evokes the
feeling of a shallow pool

＞
Furniture by KIDS DESIGN
LABO

A nursery and schoolyard that nurture independence

The increasing number of children unable to enter nurseries or kindergartens is a social concern that has gained national importance in Japan. SMW Nursery is located in a low-rise residential area not far from Tokyo. In order to eliminate long enrollment waitlists, the nursery needed to be renovated to accommodate an increased student capacity totaling 110 children.

The focus on child safety in recent years has placed several restrictions on the activities that children can participate in, making it difficult for them to play freely and be creative. Crammed schools and other "passive" learning models have also reduced their opportunities to think and act independently. To counter these restrictive trends, the grounds of SMW Nursery are designed such that they challenge children to come up with new ways to play.

Traditional nursery designs generally position the school building to the north of the plot and the schoolyard to the south. Rejecting this convention, the school building of SMW Nursery instead extends across the entire site and has been designed in an irregular shape to incorporate small gardens of different shapes and sizes along its borders. The sightlines created in these fields encourage creative play by piquing children's curiosity about what they cannot see, thus leading them to make up new games with their peers.

The design also keeps children physically active with vertical features like hills in different heights and rope nets for climbing. These elements provide greater benefits than a flat play environment.

The main rooms in the building have expansive ceilings that slope upward and outward, as well as operable sliding windows that allow abundant ventilation and natural sunlight to enter. The outdoors is brought inside to spark children's interest in nature and encourage them to play outside. Different species of trees—which include fruit trees—have been planted on the grounds, outside windows, so children can observe the seasons changing, while also taking in the other traits of nature's cycles: dried leaves that have fallen, bare branches, ripe fruits, and the insects and birds that feed on them.

The nursery's design reflects nature's changes—both inside and outside—so that children have more opportunities to make discoveries that they can share with their friends. At the same time, they develop a sense of independence as they play.

The restroom is bright and has an open atmosphere

┐
Children enjoy wading in the pool

>
The dining room connects to a small courtyard

Dining room

Classroom

A hut with rope net playing
equipment inside

> Entrance with a shoe cubby
installed neatly behind

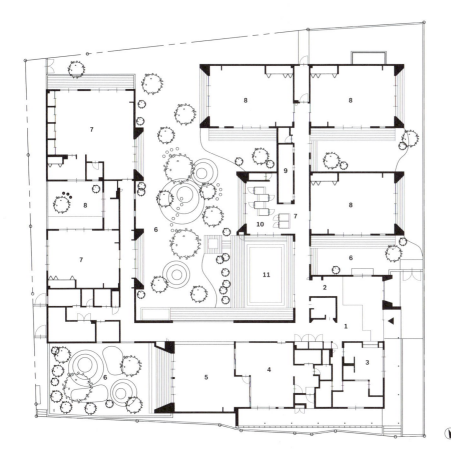

PLAN

1 Entrance
2 Library
3 Office
4 Kitchen
5 Dining room
6 Courtyard
7 Nursery for infants to
2-year-olds
8 Nursery
9 Den
10 Children's restroom
11 Swimming pool

DS Nursery

Ibaraki, Japan

COMPLETION: 2015
AREA: 15,790 ft² (1,467 m²)
PHOTOGRAPHY: Ryuji Inoue / studio BAUHAUS

Grand Prize, Ibaraki Architectural Award 2016 / Selected Architectural Designs 2016 by Architectural Institute of Japan / Japan Wood Design Award 2015 / 9th Kids Design Award

**An eco-conscious preschool
with natural scents carried in the breeze**

This nursery school sits by the sea in Ibaraki, Japan, a prefecture neighboring Tokyo, and is known for its year-round high-velocity winds. Ibaraki Prefecture also houses Japan's top offshore power generation facilities. The design of the nursery school building accounts for the area's atmospheric condition and in response tailors a one-story, square-shaped wooden building with a central courtyard. The corridor circles the entire building, allowing children to run to their heart's content without hitting a dead end. Large windows in the rooms and corridors face both the internal and external gardens and present pretty sceneries, while

∟
View of the dining room from
the courtyard

∨
The paths in the central
courtyard connect the
different rooms in the
building

windows placed higher in the building allow
natural light in.

The abundant natural light and the
generous breezes that pass through create
a positive environment and also reduce the
need for air conditioners and artificial lighting.
The courtyard is visible from anywhere in the
building and is planted with trees that flower
and bear fruit throughout the year. A deck, trail
of stepping stones, and benches encourage play
and allow children to get close to nature. With its
thoughtfully conceptualized design, DS Nursery
becomes a space where children and adults can
enjoy the enjoy the region's unique wind as well
as the changing seasons.

∧
View from the corridor to the
courtyard

＞
A blackboard wall frames the
shoe storage behind it

∧
Dining room

>
The bay windows become
play spaces for children

^

Seen from the playground, the school appears like a hollow square-shaped building

PLAN

1 Entrance
2 Office
3 Community space
4 Nursery
5 Terrace
6 Children's restroom
7 Hall
8 Nursery for infants to 2-year-olds
9 Dining room
10 Kitchen
11 Courtyard
12 Playground

<

Projecting windows at different heights create visual interest and double as seating

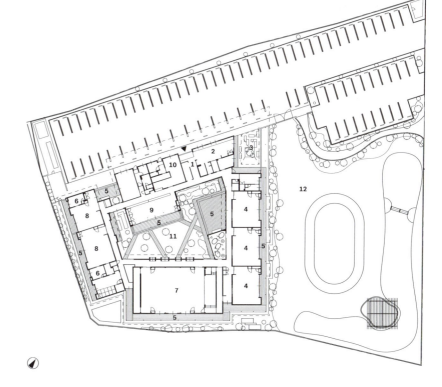

KNO Nursery

Nagasaki, Japan

COMPLETION: 2019
AREA: 6,006 ft² (558 m²)
PHOTOGRAPHY: Toshinari Soga / studio BAUHAUS

WAN Awards 2020 / Architecture Master Prize 2020 /
KDA Chairman's Award 2020 / 14th Kids Design Award

**A school building that develops
children's sensibilities with
books and reading spots**

Books help foster children's sensibilities and
awareness of things around them, and also
act as tools that encourage interaction with
their peers and the world outside. This nursery
advocates and promotes reading and book
browsing, even for children younger than a year
old. Resembling a home, this simple building
is a box-shaped wooden structure with a large
roof. Bookshelves, each displaying books on a
specific theme, have been installed throughout
the interior. For example, the bookshelf near the
kitchen has books on food and food education
and the one near the aquarium holds books on
living things. There is also a bookshelf that has
books to help energize and lift the spirits of
convalescent children.

Each bookshelf also has a fun name: the
Picture Book Hut is filled with all kinds of books;
the Big Pond Bookshelf sits right under a sunroof
with a view of the sky; and the Picture Book
Alley is lined with books for children, as well as
parents and guardians. KNO Nursery aspires
to give children the opportunity to interact with
books irrespective of where they are in the
school building.

Various read-aloud spots have also been
incorporated and include a wall-attached bench
that encircles the interior of the Picture Book
Hut, a large table with room for big groups,
stair-like spaces in classrooms, and a veranda
surrounding the building.

The design of the nursery was inspired by
the idea of "a picture book forest under a big
roof," where children can enjoy reading, talking,
and playing in their favourite spots. The features
of the school building aims to enrich the young
minds through books and other related activities.

∨
Parents and their children
reading picture books at the
entrance hall

^
Exterior view—the building
presents as a wooden
structure with a large roof,
reminiscent of a house for a
big family

v
Picture Book Hut—the books
themselves have become
part of the building

∧
Different atmospheres in
different spaces ensure
everyone can find a comfortable spot to read

>
Dark finishes in the décor
create a relaxed ambiance

<
A corridor lined with books allows children to "meet" books at every corner and turn

∨
A blackboard wall with a recessed shoe cubby area

>
The long veranda makes for a
great reading spot

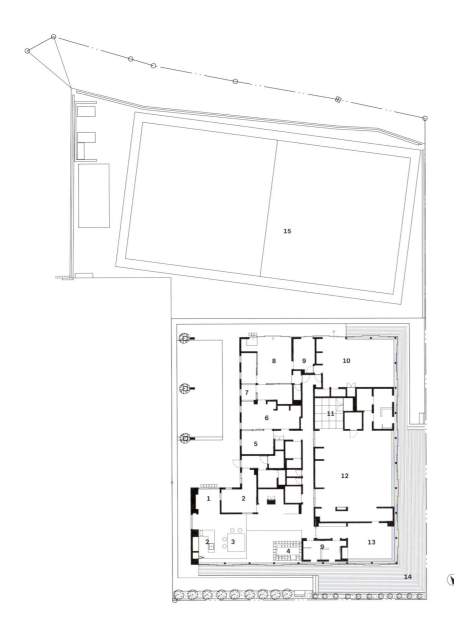

PLAN
1 Entrance
2 Kitchen
3 Parenting support room
4 Library
5 Principal's office
6 Office
7 Nurse's office
8 Sick bay
9 Children's restroom
10 After-school care room
11 Tatami space
12 Nursery for infants to
2-year-olds
13 Nursery
14 Terrace
15 Playground

ST Nursery

Saitama, Japan

COMPLETION: 2016
AREA: 12,375 ft² (1,1450 m²)
PHOTOGRAPHY: Ryuji Inoue, Toshinari Soga / studio BAUHAUS

Architizer A+Awards 2017 / Grand Prize, 5th Saitama Architectural Award / WAN Awards 2017 / Japan Wood Design Award 2017 / Good Design Award 2016 / 10th Kids Design Award

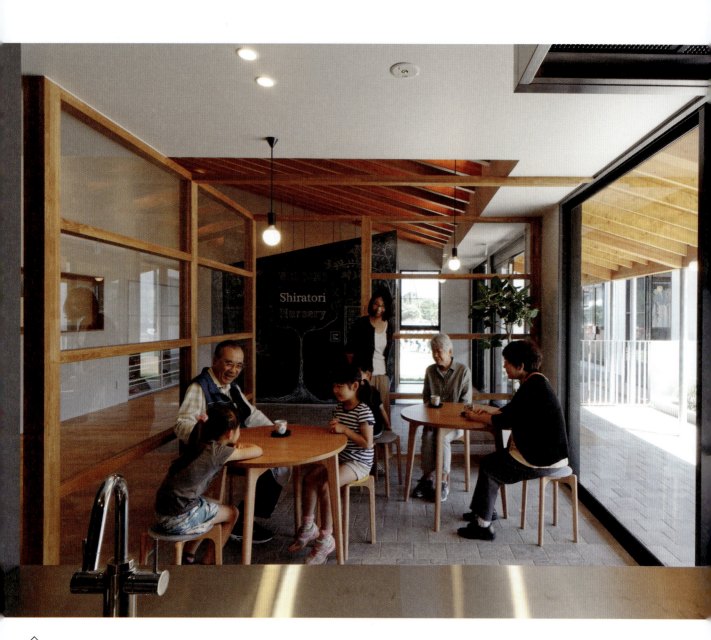

∧
A semi-public salon, where local residents casually drop by

^
Dining room with a bright
veranda

>
Exterior view

A structure of interconnected wooden huts designed to boost communication

Japan currently faces a declining birth rate, which also has resulted in children having fewer siblings. It has been noticed that bonds and camaraderie between children of different age groups in kindergartens and nurseries have also weakened, which has been attributed to weaker communication skills among the children these days.

Based on this, ST Nursery has been designed on the concept of "connection." A plan that promotes a sense of openness encourages children to connect with their environment, and specific spaces have been set up to increase opportunities to organically connect with other children and interact with people from the local community. This also supports the children's holistic development.

The school is located in an area known for a free-flowing river. The school building is constructed using interconnected wooden structures, which were inspired by wooden huts that once lined the riverbank.

The slanted rooftops allow for varying heights within the building and spaces between structures have been converted into age-specific play yards, creating a sense of rhythm and flow. The courtyard in the center is sized to foster interactions among children. The restrooms, reading corners, dining area, and other spaces used by the children are orientated toward the garden. This gives children an unobstructed view of nature and each other.

The kindergarten's design allows children to see each other and also supports teachers who work here, making it convenient for them to watch over the children. The school has been designed to facilitate a smooth operation of its facilities, as well as serve as a hub that supports good communication.

Inner courtyard

The wide corridors that circle
the library allow children to
meet each other and interact

The sunken design of the
library creates a cozy nook
that feels safe and calm

⌃
The garden zig-zags between
buildings, allowing children
of different ages from
different classes to meet
each other

PLAN
1   Entrance
2   Office
3   Nursery
4   Nursery for infants to
    2-year-olds
5   Dining room
6   Kitchen
7   Library
8   Children's restroom
9   Stage
10 Parenting support room
11 Den

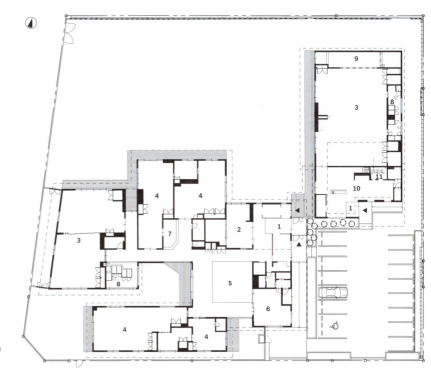

KFB Kindergarten and Nursery, Kagoshima, Japan, Photo by Ryuji Inoue

Theme 6

LANDSCAPE

Create a World for Children that Transcends Buildings

Youji no Shiro's spatial designs for children are not limited to just the buildings in question, but often also extend to the landscape to include playgrounds and other external features. However, more often than not, creating a structure on a flat, gravel-covered site disrupts the flow between the indoors and the outdoors. So, rather than simply designing flat playgrounds used for annual athletic meets, we create spaces that introduce the element of fun into everyday activities.

The space we create let children experience nature in a myriad of ways: through observing the life cycles of fruiting trees; through the scent of seasonal flowers; or even simply by playing on small hills and slopes designed into the layout. They can run, explore, or even trip over uneven spots, all of which are fundamental childhood experiences.

KFB Kindergarten and Nursery

Kagoshima, Japan

COMPLETION: 2019
AREA: 22,399 ft² (2,081 m²)
PHOTOGRAPHY: Ryuji Inoue, Toshinari Soga / studio BAUHAUS

15th Kids Design Award

Creating an uneven terrain both inside and outside of the building

KFB Kindergarten and Nursery is located in a city, at the foot of the active volcano Sakurajima in Kagoshima Prefecture, Kyushu, Japan. The Shirasu-Daichi (volcano ash) plateau in southern Kyushu that was formed over 20,000 years ago with pyroclastic flows inspired the school's design, which incorporates characteristics of the plateau's uneven terrain.

To match its design inspiration, the building is also erected on a plateau, with its surroundings dug out like a moat—the school's most distinctive feature. This unique design invites lively sessions of dynamic play among the children, who very much enjoy rolling down the slope or hiking up the incline.

The compound's playground features small hills, a rope net, and climbing spaces, among other fun highlights that promote physical activity.

Uneven surfaces are a recurring theme in this school. One such example is in the dining room, which showcases walls with uneven surfaces for climbing. In a small nook beside the entrance, a reading corner is introduced, complete with bookshelves that (you guessed it!) the children can climb. Even though a one-story structure does not usually accommodate such a variety of vertical activities, through distinct landscaping and interior refinements, a fun and inviting space that boosts imagination and supports exercise is created.

∧
The uneven terrain trains children's physical strength as they tread up and down hills

＜
A dynamic landscape extends from the building

＞
Night view

∧
Hall that has step-free
access to the outside

<
A pond in-between the
U-shaped building

∧
Lunch under the sky in the
semi-open space

＞
Dining room

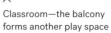
Classroom—the balcony forms another play space

^
The interior is simple but has warm atmosphere with the use of natural materials

>
Library

PLAN

1	Entrance	7	Children's restroom
2	Dining room	8	Nursery
3	Office	9	Hall
4	Nursery for infants to 2-year-olds	10	Stage
5	Courtyard	11	Library
6	Kitchen	12	Swimming pool
		13	Playground

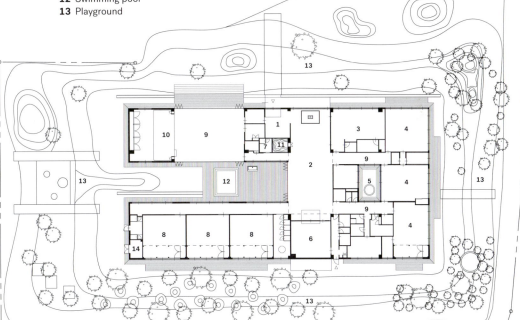

SH Kindergarten and Nursery

Toyama, Japan

COMPLETION: 2020
AREA: 17,061 ft² (1,585 m²)
PHOTOGRAPHY: Ryuji Inoue / studio BAUHAUS

Good Design Award 2022 / Architizer A+Awards 2022 / IDEA-TOPS International Space Design Award 2021 / Silver Award, WAN Awards 2021 / 15th Kids Design Award

˄
A mountain-like landscape
created inside the building

^
All the components are
reminiscent of natural
elements—caves, pond, hills
and different terrains

A school building inspired by natural terrains that kindle children's natural curiosity

The Japanese Alps, also known as the "the roof of Japan," cut right through the middle of the main island of Honshu. The grounds of the newly built SH Kindergarten and Nursery overlook the beautiful Tateyama Mountain Range, which makes up part of the Japanese Alps. The Tateyama Range offers both a gentle trail for beginners, as well as a steep, rugged path for experienced climbers. The view and flora, which includes plants, trees, and flowers, vary in each trail. These richly diverse climbing trails inspired the design of this school building.

The interior of the building has ten play areas: a confined hideaway, like a rugged rock cave, a corridor similar to a tunnel that urges children to explore what lies ahead; rope nets that encourage them to climb, a hill-like spot with a view of the kitchen and dining area on the first floor, and a relaxed reading space that resembles a pond.

The play areas mentally and physically stimulate children and motivate them to make discoveries, like how they would do so on an adventurous trip on the mountains. We believe that the diverse "terrains" inside the school building will help nurture and shape children's intellect. It is also hoped that the children who spend time at the school will develop an affinity for, and a deeper understanding of the Tateyama Mountain Range, which is a symbol of the town.

⌃
Children can get an overhead
view of the dining area from
a glass-walled space above

> A cave-like space with a
diagonal ceiling

∨

Library

‹
A tunnel-like corridor

^

Nets above the corridor
make for an interesting and
fun play experience

‹

Every corner presents opportunities for exploratory play

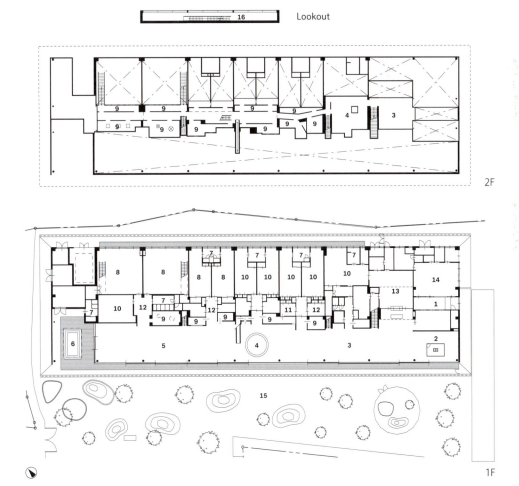

Lookout

16

2F

1F

PLAN

1 Entrance
2 Community lounge
3 Dining room
4 Library
5 Hall
6 Swimming pool
7 Children's restroom
8 Nursery
9 Den
10 Nursery for infants to
   2-year-olds
11 Tea ceremony room
12 Counseling room
13 Kitchen
14 Office
15 Playground
16 Observation deck

HN Nursery

Kanagawa, Japan

COMPLETION: 2017
AREA: 6,167 ft² (573 m²)
PHOTOGRAPHY: Toshinari Soga / studio BAUHAUS

IAI Special Jury Award 2018 / Architizer A+Awards 2018 / International Design Media Award 2018 / Japan Wood Design Award 2018 / 12th Kids Design Award

A building and furniture designed by walking in a child's shoes

HN Nursery was founded by a parent who wanted to raise his/her children among rich nature. To fulfil this, the nursery is conceptualized to be a space where children can be stimulated by nature throughout the day and be excited to play among it.

Playing among nature also serves to develop creativity and awareness. When children play indoors, they often do so with factory-made toys already assembled to fit their design and purpose, limiting flexibility in their use. When children play in nature, however, changes of seasons, the weather, and natural colors and textures, plus the many sights, sounds, and scents of the elements within the landscape weave a truly vivid experience for them that is not easily forgotten. In the outdoors, children are exposed to a host of details, such as the warmth of the sun, the texture of the earth, the smell of a flower, and the color of the sky. The school, is therefore, designed such that the children can feel nature at every corner, and fill their day with nature-centered activities that enable them to make memorable discoveries and learn to think and rationalize independently.

Among the design details selected to tailor a nature-focused environment are a big banyan tree planted in the nursery room—which tests the children's tree-climbing skills—and a glass roof that frames moving portraits of clouds that float by. In the playground, a big, 16-foot (5-meter) hill enables creative games of rolling, sliding, and flopping about. Even infants get in on the fun as they crawl about and enjoy the feel of grass under them.

The building is home to a
lush, thriving banyan tree,
which the children enjoy
climbing

∧
A hilly garden planted with trees cultivates a love for nature as children play and explore and build positive experiences

<
A transparent roof over the dining area, together with views of refreshing greenery creates a feeling of being outdoors

∧
A spacious hall

∨
View from the garden

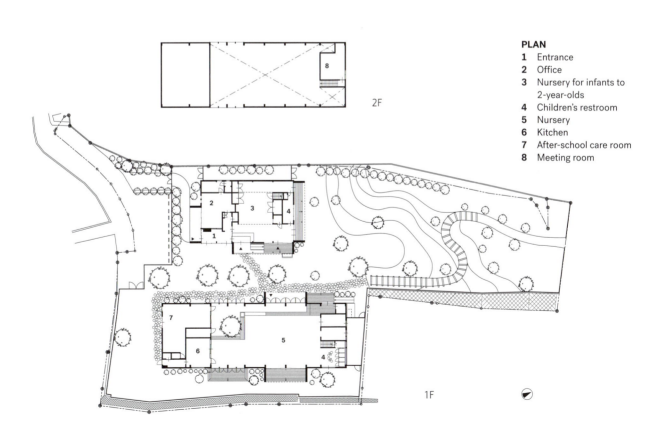

PLAN
1 Entrance
2 Office
3 Nursery for infants to
   2-year-olds
4 Children's restroom
5 Nursery
6 Kitchen
7 After-school care room
8 Meeting room

2F

1F

ibg School, Beijing, China

LARGE-SCALE PROJECTS

See Through the Eyes of a Child

Most newly established and upcoming kindergartens in many emerging residential areas in Japan, as well as overseas can accommodate 400 or more children. Such large-scale preschools must be designed from both a micro and macro perspective. This entails a thorough understanding of how children spend their time in classrooms, and how they interact with their peers and adults. The surrounding landscape must also be considered from a broad perspective. Focusing on the broader perspective leads to architectural designs that focus on efficiency, and the creation of spaces in which children can feel at ease. When designing for large structures, it is always good practice to incorporate a variety of spaces that allow children to interact in small groups, stop and play, or even hide, in the event that they do not feel like socializing.

ibg School

Beijing, China

COMPLETION: 2019
AREA: 33,325 ft² (3,096 m²)
PHOTOGRAPHY: Hibino Sekkei

A large preschool with natural elements that fascinate children

The environments within kindergartens are known to stimulate children's senses through various experiences. These experiences are all the more valuable when they occur in a natural environment. In this project, a three-story building in Beijing, China, is renovated and turned into

a kindergarten with planted trees and natural materials, such as wood and stone.

The main features of the preschool are a lush courtyard and a rooftop playground; it is expected that the insects and birds that visit the tree-filled lawn, plus the changing seasons that bring different temperatures and tree foliage, will pique the children's curiosity and create a

colorful range of engaging moments that can be enriching learning experiences. Varying ground levels in the courtyard also encourage various forms of physical activity and exercise so that little limbs experience the needed core movement to help build muscle and strength.

The nursery rooms are made as functional as possible to accommodate a large number of students. A simple décor helps to highlight the rich, green landscape of the garden and also accentuates the many natural elements that surround the school, such as the fragrance of the plants and flowers, and the sounds of the elements, like wind and rain.

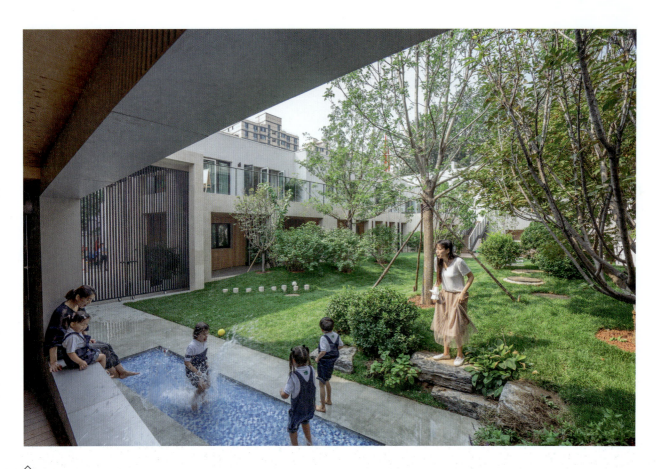

∧
Children playing in the pond

＞
A part of the indoor courtyard is boarded, to be a multipurpose space that can be used for various occasions

^
Children can also eat on the
veranda as an alternative
dining space

∧
A varied courtyard

<
Classroom with built-in
shelves

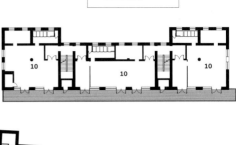

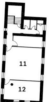

3F

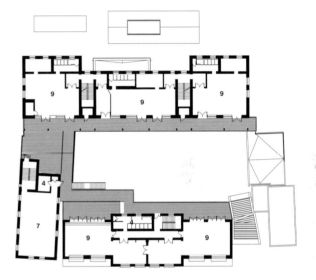

2F

PLAN
1 Entrance hall
2 Nursery for children 2 to 3 years old
3 Dining room
4 Children's restroom
5 Library
6 Event hall
7 Atelier
8 Kitchen
9 Nursery for children 4 to 5 years old
10 Nursery for children 5 to 6 years old
11 Office
12 Meeting room

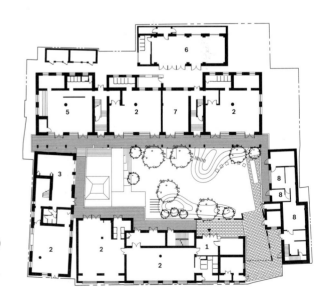

1F

KO Kindergarten

Ehime, Japan

COMPLETION: 2019
AREA: 29,170 ft² (2,710 m²)
PHOTOGRAPHY: Ryuji Inoue / studio BAUHAUS, Kosuke Tamura

IDEA-TOPS International Space Design Award 2020 /
13th Kids Design Award

A space that presents fun ways for children to exercise and interact

There is a growing social concern about the lack of exercise among children in Japan and their declining physical strength. The cause of this is often cited as being the increased traffic, which has restricted children's movement outside of the home.

In response to this and to help children still enjoy physical activities, the design of this kindergarten transforms a large-scale building into a space that encourages more than 450 children to exercise, even while they are indoors.

Classrooms are placed on the first and second floors, with a large, open hall in the center on both floors. The classrooms and staircases are also arranged such that gaps are created in numerous spots and turned into play areas. Other play elements in the hall include an inverted dome—inside which children can run around and chase each other—rooms connected by ladders and slides that ascend and descend, and a space where they can hurl balls at different shapes on the wall. This layout not only offers fun ways to exercise, but also ensures that children can easily communicate with peers of all ages across the large hall.

˅

An indoor playground that utilizes the gap between the mezzanine and the floor below

A large hall is placed in the
center of the building

Entrance hall

A ladder that connects to a
secret playroom

Nursery

A play area with a rope net
play structure

A play area with a climbing
pole

Children having fun at the
play area with a beveled floor

⟨
Playground with a small hill

M2F

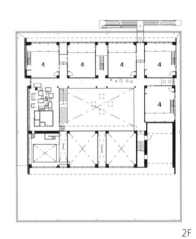

2F

PLAN
1 Entrance
2 Office
3 Nursery for infants to
  2-year-olds
4 Nursery room
5 Children's restroom
6 Den
7 Hall
8 Playground

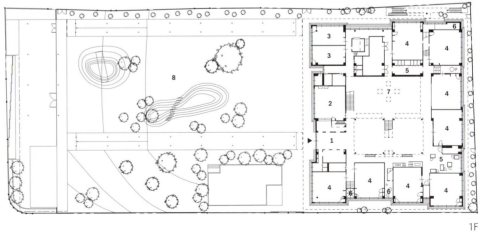

1F

Chapter

02

Clients

Speak

KIDS SMILE LABO, Kanagawa, Japan, Photo by Keisuke Fukamizu

KIDS SMILE LABO

Kanagawa, Japan

A nursery school redefines yard-less environments

KIDS SMILE LABO is a nursery school with a simple and unpretentious composition that allows children to feel at one with nature despite its urban location.

It is located in the middle of the city, near a large rail terminal in Kanagawa Prefecture, Japan, not too far from Tokyo. The nursery occupies the entire second floor of Hibino Sekkei's annex office, with office facilities located on the third floor, along with our restaurant, 2343 FOOD LABO.

Hibino Sekkei has designed more than 500 preschool facilities in the past, but KIDS SMILE LABO is the first to be owned and managed by us as well.

In an open floor plan abound with elevations and transformations, the center features a tiered platform resembling a stage, surrounded by a cozy atelier, bookshelves, and a bathroom with mirrored walls. The space also has a room for infants to nap and play in with minimal noise disturbance from the other areas in the center. While the facility lacks a schoolyard, children can still play outside at a nearby riverside, irrespective of the weather.

There are many benefits to be had within the building as well. For example, 2343 FOOD LABO emphasizes the use of local ingredients on its menu, as well as in the meals provided for the children, to promote the use of locally grown produce that is fresher and more nutritious as the ingredients don't travel long distances to get to the end consumer; it is also more sustainable and results in less wastage from food spoilage. Through the meals prepared at 2343 FOOD LABO, the school strives to teach children about healthy eating.

KIDS SMILE LABO is a product of Youji no Shiro's extensive research on the spatial design and management of childcare facilities. It is a treat to children's senses and serves as a reliable pillar for families in their busy urban lifestyles. Truly, this nursery is a Hibino Sekkei Youji no Shiro original.

COMPLETION: 2021
AREA: 3,660 ft² (340 m²)
PHOTOGRAPHY: Keisuke Fukamizu

International Design Media Awards 2021

>
A secret nook behind the atelier space

∧
Nursery

>
A child enjoying the swing in
the nursery

Kaoru Matsushita
Principal, KIDS SMILE LABO

Takashi Mori
Vice Principal, KIDS SMILE LABO

We want our space to show people the limitless potential of urban nurseries.

∧
A blackboard wall frames the kitchen counter

Q   KIDS SMILE LABO uses an entire floor of an office building. The space is almost uninterrupted: Kids of all ages learn and interact in one open room. This feels like quite a bold design choice for a nursery.

A   Splitting up the space according to class and age would have imposed further restrictions on the limited space. We felt that an open, one-room floor plan would ensure that the school feels spacious to our children aged 2 to 5 years old. They can move freely, even when indoors. We're pleased with our decision.

Q The "dead" spaces and different-sized steps inside KIDS SMILE LABO make good play areas for kids. The facility's architecture was designed by Hibino Sekkei's Youji no Shiro and has been specifically tailored to promote children's learning. Given its success, it's probable that similar features will be actively incorporated in many other projects going forward. As the chief of operations, did you have any safety concerns?

A We deliberately aspired to create a space you wouldn't typically find in nurseries. When the school first opened, the staff, including myself, were sometimes unsure about how to proceed. But over time, the children learned how to utilize the space and we also learned to anticipate things. Frankly speaking, I had my doubts about the space being "user-friendly" [laughs]. When kids climbed on the shelves, for example, I thought: "This seems dangerous." It was sometimes difficult to decide—should I stop them or just watch over them? However, I still feel it's important for children to discover for themselves how to use different places.

Library

Children create freely in the atelier

∧
Children having lunch with friends

∧
A fun mirror wall wraps around the children's restroom

＞
Storage shelves are incorporated at the children's eye levels

∧
Nursery

＞
Toddlers' nap time

Q **This nursery occupies the entire floor of an office building near to a major rail terminal. There's no schoolyard and no balconies either. How did you resolve the drawback of not having an outdoor space that is often common in urban nurseries?**

A When people hear that a children's nursery is located in an office building, they tend to envision children crammed into a confined space. Hibino Sekkei's vision of creating a world-class urban nursery dispels this image.

Our nursery's interior evokes a forest with its wide use of plants. The space imparts a sense oneness with nature, despite being indoors. There are plants all over the nursery, and our children love watering them! Also, members of our staff walk with the children to the nearby riverside every day, where they play to their hearts' content. So, even though we don't have a schoolyard, our children learn and discover new things from nature on a daily basis.

Cities are going to see many more nurseries without schoolyards in the future. We hope KIDS SMILE LABO can serve as a role model for them.

Q   **KIDS SMILE LABO is also dedicated to food education. Your meals are provided by 2343 FOOD LABO, also run by Hibino Sekkei.**

A   Food education is one of our nursery's appeals. More than a few children who come to us have imbalanced or sparse diets. At the nursery, they get delicious food made using seasonal ingredients, along with plenty of exercise. Together, both these aspects improve their health and nutrition. Sometimes, I get drawn in watching the children munch away. Turns out, the food is just as delicious for adults! [laughs] Kids are shown ingredients from the kitchen counter, always tastefully arranged. Our culinary staff work hard to source the best ingredients, even seeking out local organic farm produce; they are always experimenting to determine what works best for the children and what appeals to them.

∧
Lunch time

∧
The brightly lit restroom is clean and inviting

‹
Shoe storage

Q   KIDS SMILE LABO seems like a great place to work at as well, from an adult's perspective.

A   Our staff definitely enjoys the atmosphere that fills the nursery; it keeps them energized while they work. The space's energy meshes well with the nursery's operations. It ensures that the kids are treated well, and the adults are engaged every day.

An indoor garden

Q   Finally, could you both share on your favorite spots in the school?

A   Personally, I like the wide steps of the tiered stage area. The plants all around put me at ease, and you can see trains from the window. The space is characteristic of our nursery's vibe. (Mori)

I'm particularly drawn to the role-play space behind the atelier. Newly admitted students, Newly admitted children, especially babies less than a year old, generally find it difficult to relax in a huge room. The space, nestled between the shelves and windows, has a naturally calming effect: despite not being told to, they take a toy from a shelf and start playing. They first play alone and then gradually learn to play with their new friends. (Matsushita)

∧
Children looking out to the
surrounding town

⟩
The river near the nursery
makes for an engaging
playground for children

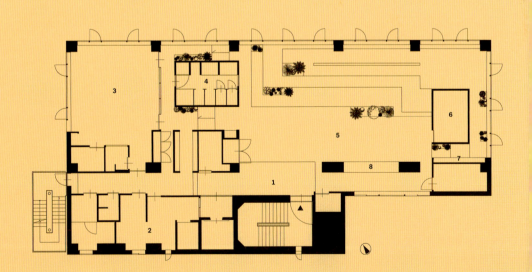

PLAN
1 Entrance hall
2 Office
3 Nursery for infants to
   1-year-olds
4 Children's restroom
5 Nursery
6 Atelier
7 Library
8 Children's kitchen

YM Nursery

Tottori, Japan

Transforming early childhood spaces with natural architecture

The location of this school is set among Japan's Tottori Prefecture's rich abundant nature, specifically Yumi-ga-hama beach and Ōyama Mountain. Together with the new building, the furniture, fixtures, and various other fittings and accessories have also been designed to match the concept of the nursery.

It was priority in the design to create a space that could remind children of the magnificent nature of the local region. For both the exterior and interior of the building, plenty of local wood and stone were used. Traditional handicrafts belonging to this region were also specifically incorporated in the design, such as kasuri textile, and kilns for ceramic-making. For example, the lampshade in each room that doubles as the signage for the room is made of kasuri textile that has been weaved into an original pattern to graphically represent the name of the room. Modern design has been fused into traditional crafts in many ways.

The space is imbued with a natural atmosphere by using solid wood and leather for the furniture, which has been made from the pelts of various animals. In this nursery, children step on rocks, feel them against the soles of their feet, rub their cheeks against the wood, and enjoy the texture of the leather against their palms. Through their time spent in the nursery, they learn the comfort of real, natural materials, and the beauty of products derived from the nature that surrounds their local community.

COMPLETION: 2018
AREA: 12,335 ft² (1,146 m²)
PHOTOGRAPHY: Ryuji Inoue / studio BAUHAUS, Toru Kometani

Goldreed Industrial Design Award 2020 / Finalist, World Architecture Festival 2019 / Bronze, A' Design Award 2019 / Best Humanistic Care, IAI Design AWARD 2018 / China Good Design Award 2018

⌐
Entrance hall

＞
A shallow pond gathers water when it rains

^
View of the dining hall from
the garden

^
Spacious dining room

<
Exterior view

Hitoshi Sato
Principal, YM Nursery

> The natural materials around us give both the children and adults room to breathe, emotionally speaking.

Q What prompted you to rebuild the nursery?

A The building was originally a public nursery school. We've been running it since it was privatized. The nursery had been first built nearly forty years ago. At the time, day care for infants aged 1 and below was not common. The place felt rundown, cramped, and behind the times in many aspects.

Q What were your reasons for requesting Youji no Shiro to design the reconstruction?

A In our search for a team that would create a superbly designed school building, we met with several companies. Youji no Shiro, in particular, had a wealth of imaginative ideas. Their design concept "Treasuring the Character of the Land through Architecture" made a lasting impression.

Youji no Shiro envisioned a nursery that incorporates local materials and also blends into the surroundings yet stands out. Their ideas are now a reality: our building uses locally sourced stone, wood, and kasuri textiles.

< A rope-net playing equipment and a slide

Q   What were your first impressions of the new building?

A   The kids and their parents were delighted: "Wow! It's so pretty!" many commented excitedly. We were pleased, especially with the interiors. It uses a lot of wood, which is easy on the eyes, and it smells nice too. Our combined dining room and hall has a solid wood flooring and floor-to-ceiling windows that face the schoolyard. The interior is filled with natural sunlight, creating a warm and inviting atmosphere.

Our employees spend most of their day here, so the environment plays an important role in keeping their spirits up. I don't know if there's a causal relationship with the architecture, but our children seem more at ease and tolerant in the new building. That's true for us adults too. The high ceilings, the natural materials, and the beautiful local scenery—the space gives us room to breathe, emotionally speaking.

∨
Signages are made of traditional local kasuri textile

∧
Corridor on the second floor

Q   Most of the building's furniture was designed by KIDS DESIGN LABO. How did it feel about the solid wood furniture?

A   The furniture is an integral yet unobtrusive part of YM Nursery. The solid wood is easy to maintain: if an area gets noticeably dirty, we just sand it out. We followed Youji no Shiro's suggestion to use backless stools in the dining hall. In addition to their sleek design, the stools have a strong functional advantage: children have to make a conscious effort to sit up because the chairs don't have backrests, and this helps strengthen their core.

Q The building has rugged stone surfaces, steep slides, even a wood-burning stove—all elements which might be perceived as dangerous by a typical nursery or kindergarten. What made you decide to incorporate these elements?

A You often hear stories about people getting rid of playground equipment from parks and schools under the pretext of them being "dangerous." Sure, doing this reduces risks, but at the same time, it robs children of learning opportunities. I believe a school needs uneven surfaces and steep steps to give children opportunities to think for themselves as they play. Granted, some situations are dangerous—it is important to be cautious in these cases—but as far as possible, we don't want to restrict children's activities. YM Nursery is grounded in the relationship of trust that our staff consciously build with the children and their parents.

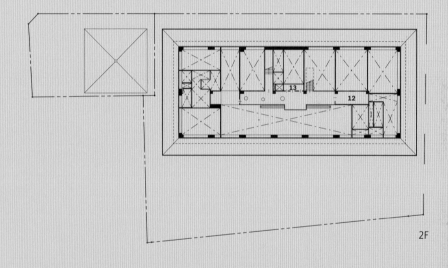

2F

PLAN
1 Entrance
2 Office
3 Kitchen
4 Nursery
5 Children's restroom
6 Dining room / hall
7 Nursery for infants to 2-year-olds
8 Inner terrace
9 Swimming pool
10 Playground
11 After-school care room
12 Library
13 Den

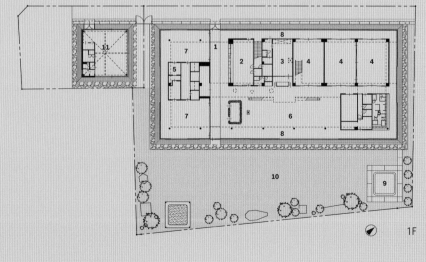

1F

WZY Kindergarten

Guiyang, China

A kindergarten design that fosters lasting engagements

WZY Kindergarten is situated in a housing development zone in Guiyang, China. The kindergarten is approximately 12,917 square feet (1,200 square meters), with a 6,458-square-foot (600-square-meter) terrace, and is on the third floor of a newly constructed building. The client is one of the leading companies in Montessori education in Guiyang. The interior design of the kindergarten reflects the company's education philosophy and features elements true to Guiyang's nature-rich locality.

The Montessori method of education originated in Italy and is founded on the belief that children have an innate ability to foster their own growth. Prominent individuals like Jeff Bezos and Larry Page received a Montessori education. This method of learning emphasizes free and spontaneous activities and the use of distinctive teaching tools that encourage critical thinking.

The design incorporates the building and its surroundings as teaching tools. For example, the outer walls are used to teach the concepts of numerals and quantities. A lush playground connects to the dining area and a reading corner with special features. School designs that incorporate educational concepts inside and outside the building can be exciting for children and encourage discoveries, independent thinking, and diverse experiences. As much as possible, locally sourced materials were used for the building.

When this interior design project was completed, the client offered us an architecture design project for another of their nurseries, which is underway at the moment. The architecture will be realized to include a garden inspired by the hilly topography of Guiyang, as well as indoor and outdoor playgrounds that evoke the local topography.

⌐
Library corner and rope net
playing equipment at far end

COMPLETION: 2019
AREA: 12,917 ft² (1,200 m²)
PHOTOGRAPHY: Hibino Sekkei

>
Dining room

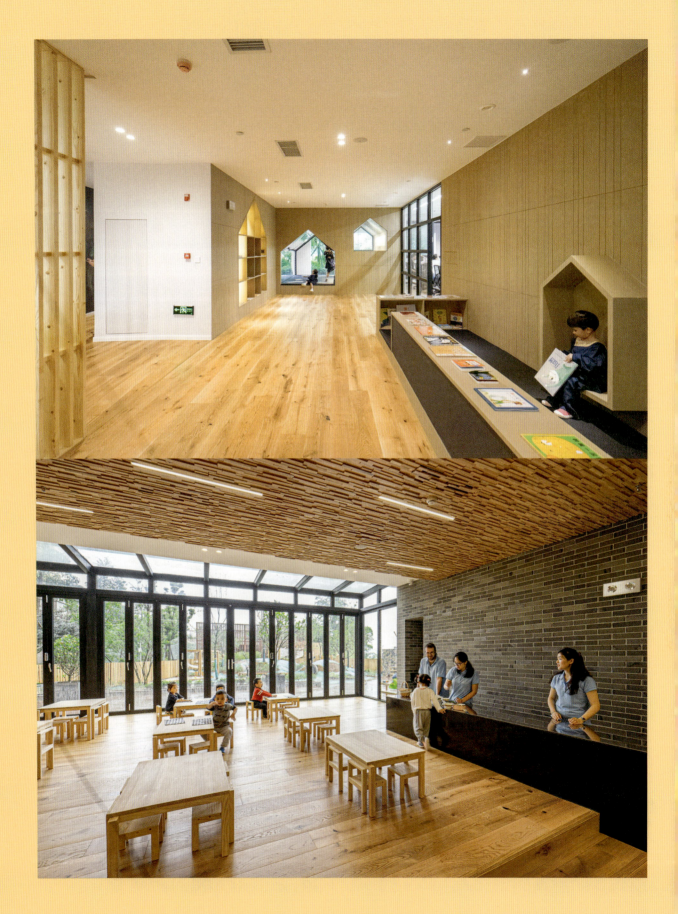

Gu Zhengye
Chairman and Founder, WZY Kindergarten

Sometimes the kids love the kindergarten too much, which can cause problems! [laughs]

Q   **You requested Youji no Shiro to design your kindergarten. What was your rationale?**

A   While I was researching possible architecture firms to take on this project, I came across photos of Youji no Shiro's previous works. Their design for D1 Kindergarten was particularly impressive. They had designed an open floor plan that allowed children to run around freely, and had installed full-length glass walls that let children look into the kitchen and other rooms. Youji no Shiro's designs are perfectly suited for children; plus, they are known for their excellent quality. Our team in-charge of the redesign was convinced that Youji no Shiro would be the best choice.

⌄
Nursery—the glassed-in space in the center houses the children's restroom

∧
Carefully designed signages

Q   When you set out to build your kindergarten, did you have a shared vision with the designers?

A   Conventional designs for kindergartens in China tend to use cushioned walls and flooring and safety covers on corners, placing excessive emphasis on safety.

While this is good thinking and appreciated, it's also important that children develop the skill of judging danger for themselves and learn from getting injured—these are critical skills that even we as adults use.

This concept is truly visible in the space designed by Youji no Shiro, with its uneven surfaces and hideouts. They might appear "dangerous" in a certain sense, but they are also opportunities for children to learn and discover. Our shared overarching concept gave me the confidence to entrust Youji no Shiro with the design process.

^
Dining room

>
Hall

Q **That's a very progressive way of thinking: for not over-prioritizing safety and regarding injuries as opportunities for children to learn and discover. Do parents and employees understand your perspective?**

A We invested a lot of energy in educating our teachers and staff about our vision for the space and its design. I was passionate about communicating these things, along with our educational philosophy. Our employees genuinely understand our message, and the teachers are great at relaying it to the parents.

But what convinces the parents and staff more than anything else is the growth of the children; it's by leaps and bounds. The development of their academic and physical skills is visible in this pleasant environment. The kids love the school: they say they want to stay here forever, which makes things difficult for the teachers! [laughs] I hope our school can change the conventional wisdom of kindergartens.

Q A few years have passed since WZY Kindergarten opened in 2019. You're also having a new one built, again based on a design by Youji no Shiro.

A We're planning an educational facility that includes both a kindergarten and an elementary school. Our aim is to contribute to improving the quality of education in China. We believe that Hibino Sekkei and Youji no Shiro are the best partners to design spaces in line with our goals.

┌ ∧
Interior view of the new project (rendering image)

‹
Exterior view of the new project (rendering image)

PLAN

1	Piloti	**8**	Corridor
2	Entrance	**9**	Music & P.E. room
3	Office	**10**	Den
4	Dining room	**11**	Library
5	Kitchen	**12**	Terrace
6	Nursery	**13**	Playground
7	Children's restroom		

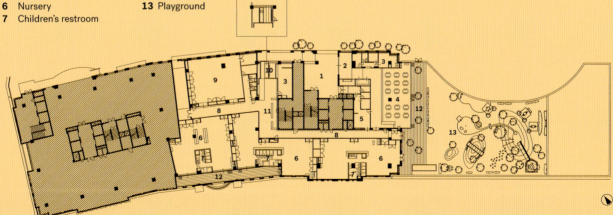

SDL Nursery

Guangzhou, China

Architectural support to foster growth and business success

This project designs the interiors of a nursery school located inside a metropolitan high-rise building. Given the location of the site, and with having the school being situated indoors in a building, there were limited opportunities for contact with nature. The design thus sought to incorporate various plants and greenery to create a sense of openness.

The first floor of the school has a reception area and an exhibit space. The area is spacious with a high ceiling and makes an ideal venue for parents and guardians to leisurely spend their time there when visiting the school. On the second floor, the far end—which is also the quietest and sunniest spot—is turned into a space for infants, and the front area is turned into classrooms loosely separated by low partition walls. The partition walls can be adjusted according to the number of children and other classroom requirements. They also allow teachers to view the entire area, facilitating staff collaborations across classroom boundaries. The walls can also be used to create small spaces where children can feel at ease. It was essential to ensure a flexible design plan that safely utilized the limited area to meet the dynamic educational needs of the school.

The third floor is divided into three areas: a space for activities—such as art and reading—a multipurpose area that opens into the terrace, and an office. The use of glass and low partitions create a sense of space and visibility. The multipurpose area has been envisioned as a space to serve children, parents and guardians, and teachers, who can also use the room to conduct meetings or take breaks.

SDL Nursery does away with creating restrictions based on where the children and their families come from. Characterized by social significance and a desire to offer a wide range of educational nurturing, the space is now an exemplar for other nursery schools.

⌐
Library

>
Café space

COMPLETION: 2020
AREA: 13,993 ft² (1,300 m²)
PHOTOGRAPHY: Ivan Cho

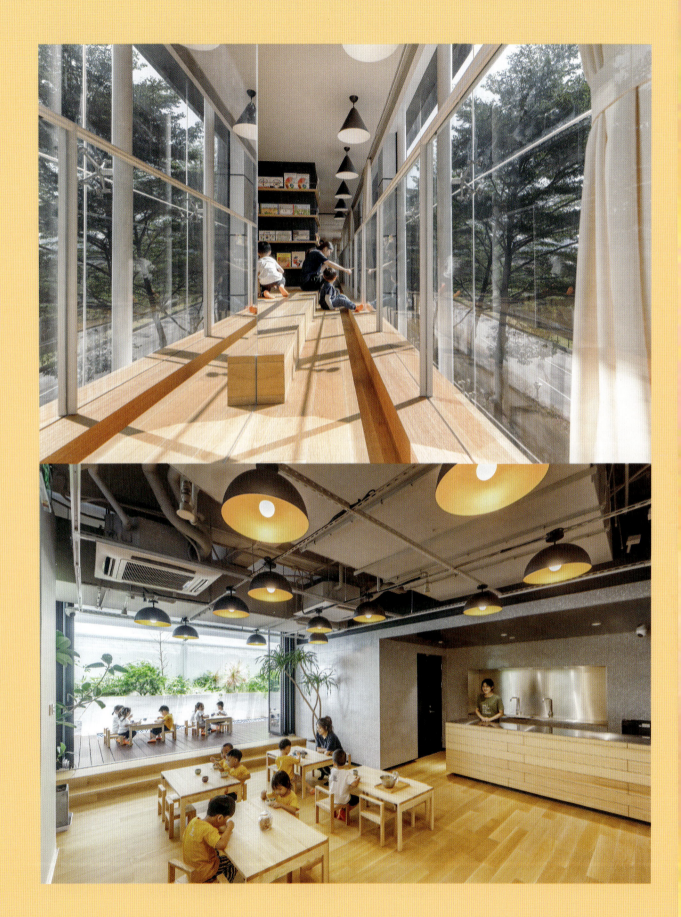

< Library

WORDS FROM THE CLIENT

Chen Zhixuan

Founder and CEO of Xiaoxiao Education Ltd

Investor of SDL Nursery

 Youji no Shiro makes the perfect partner for businesses passionate about nursery and kindergarten design.

> Entrance hall

Rooftop terrace

Q **First, could you give us an overview of your nursery? Why did you engage Youji no Shiro for this project?**

A SDL Nursery is located on the third floor of an office building in urban Guangzhou. I've been running nurseries in other locations, but I wanted this one to be built differently; a "high-class" institution with top-tier education. This goal led me to partner with Youji no Shiro to design the space. I saw a few of their works on the internet. They use simple design tones and plenty of natural materials.

Also, their concepts are aligned with this guiding principle: "What does it really mean for a space to be designed with children in mind?" It really got me thinking. The public tends to think that early childhood education facilities should be colorful. But that's an adult's interpretation of "child-friendly" or "child-like." I've long suspected that children innately prefer natural colors. Youji no Shiro shares this belief.

Q SDL Nursery is located inside an office building in a large city. How do you feel about the completed space?

A Since the space isn't very big, Youji no Shiro recommended using low partitions that were 3.9 feet (1.2 meters) in height. I was initially concerned that the children's voices would carry over the partitions, making the space noisy, but Youji no Shiro has a long track record and so I trusted them. When we officially began using the space, the children got used to it in a flash. It was the adults who took longer to get used to it! [laughs] That's because we're accustomed to classrooms being separated by walls. I made the effort to train my employees, educating them about the intention underlying the space while helping them understand the significance of their work.

>
The children enjoy a full view of the kitchen and can watch meals being prepared

<
Children's restroom

Q   How do the parents react?

A   Overwhelmingly positively! The parents are especially pleased with the kitchen and bathrooms. Our nursery's kitchen has full-length glass walls so that everyone can see how the meals are being cooked. In addition to it being aesthetically appealing, this transparency helps build parents' trust in the safety and quality of the meals we provide. Our hut-shaped restroom stalls are also quite popular. The restroom uses high-quality equipment, and we keep it super clean: the kids even use it to play hide and seek! Parents become increasingly curious once they have experienced the superior quality of the space: "What do they teach kids here?" they ask.

Running a nursery takes more than space or enthusiasm. There are several aspects like costs, branding, planning, budgets, and working conditions. Public nurseries can reach full capacity without much effort. This is not true for private nurseries. Youji no Shiro understands this challenge perfectly, and advised us every step of the way. For businesses passionate about early childhood education, they make a fantastic partner.

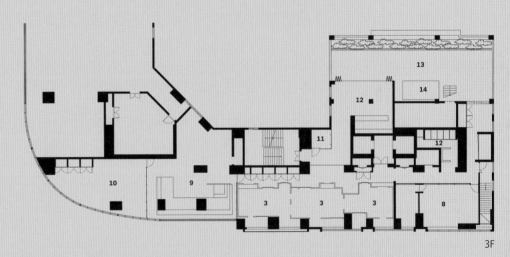

3F

PLAN
1   Entrance
2   Nursery for infants to
     2-year-olds
3   Nursery
4   Meeting room
5   Hall
6   Kitchen
7   Children's restroom
8   Hibino Sekkei China
     office
9   Library
10 Classroom
11 Office
12 Café
13 Outdoor classroom
14 Climbing wall

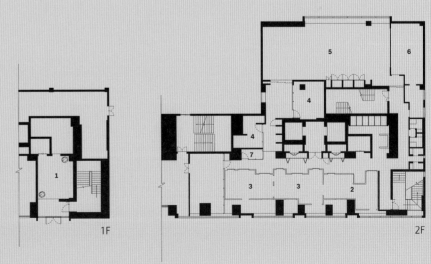

1F

2F

KR Kindergarten and Nursery

Hokkaido, Japan

KS Primary School

Hokkaido, Japan

Various personalized spaces for each child's well-being

KR Kindergarten and Nursery is a certified center for early childhood education and care in Sapporo, the capital of Japan's Hokkaido Prefecture. The facility was constructed on the grounds of a forest park, a green island in a suburban sea. The school's design inherits the memory and history of the land by utilizing the terrain and preserving the verdant forest rather than destroying it. We envisioned a nursery where children could grow up playing in the forest, just like those of generations past.

KR Kindergarten and Nursery sits on a slope, but instead of leveling the grounds, we made a conscientious decision to incorporate the existing terrain. The building's interior follows the incline: children climb stairs and go down slides, as if they're playing in the woods. There are several elevated features across the facility, which includes a tiered library. Children can also gaze down through glass barriers at the sunken kitchen and office. Every day in school is an adventure full of discoveries and games in a forest.

KS Primary School was a space acquired by the client. As keen proponents of sustainability, we opted to preserve the old school building in our renovation and redesign. We deliberately incorporate rough finishes that would expose some of the building's original material, such as undressed concrete, to offer students the opportunity to learn about their schoolhouse.

The architecture of both KR Kindergarten and Nursery and KS Primary School is grounded in stimulating of children's curiosity. Both these spaces spark active communication and physical play. Our client, K.T., is a former Japanese professional baseball player. The well-known infielder also played Major League Baseball in the United States. Prior to his retiring from playing professionally, K.T. sought Youji no Shiro's counsel, expressing his desire to build a private school for childhood education from the ground up. Undoubtedly, an outsider such as K.T. has the potential to revolutionize education with new practices and approaches.

KR KINDERGARTEN AND NURSERY
COMPLETION: 2021
DESIGN TEAM: Hibino Sekkei Youji no Shiro
TOTAL FLOOR AREA: 7,524 ft² (699 m²)
PHOTOGRAPHY: Toshinari Soga / studio BAUHAUS

KS PRIMARY SCHOOL
COMPLETION: 2021
DESIGN TEAM: Hibino Sekkei Youji no Shiro
TOTAL FLOOR AREA: 39,557 ft² (3,675 m²)
PHOTOGRAPHY: Toshinari Soga / studio BAUHAUS

┐
Exterior view of KR Kindergarten and Nursery

⟩
Library of KS Primary School

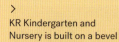

> KR Kindergarten and
> Nursery is built on a bevel

WORDS FROM THE CLIENT

K.T.

President, KS Primary School

For places where children spend a lot of time, we have to get creative about stimulating their senses.

< Bookshelves along the
staircase

∨ Hall of KR Kindergarten and
Nursery

Q   Mr. K.T., you were originally a professional baseball player. Have you always had an interest in education?

A   I've been devoted to baseball since I was a young boy. Education and the broader society weren't really on my mind. That changed during the two years I was playing Major League Baseball in the United States. I was given the opportunity to visit Venezuela. At the time, Venezuela's education standards weren't especially high. Crime rates were high, though. The boundary between good and bad considerably differed from that in Japan. Also, I noticed people's English comprehension wasn't so good in Central and South America. That was the moment I realized how a little education could change a lot.

My wife and I had a child after that, and we returned to Japan. I thought about how I wanted my own child to learn, and so I began exploring and understanding education for the sake of education. My desire to contribute to the education of Hokkaido's children comes from my deep sense of gratitude I have had toward the region ever since I played professionally with a Hokkaido team.

> Design elements in the nursery, like this slide and overhead ladder, utilize the undulations of the site

Q   Between the kindergarten/nursery and primary school, you have been engaged in the education of children for over twelve years now. That's quite a long period.

A   The period from infancy to 12 years old is critical in laying the groundwork for a person's character. The environment, as well as how you spend your time, and with whom, greatly influences the rest of your life. I feel my job carries a big responsibility, but it is also deeply satisfying and meaningful.

^
Steps gently divide the space
in the nursery

^
The open kitchen in
KS Primary School helps
children to get interested in
their food

<
Windows placed high floods
the children's restroom with
natural light

Q   **You requested Youji no Shiro to design the spaces of both your facilities. What was your rationale?**

A   Excitement is the biggest motivator for children to learn. I sensed not just excitement but also warmth and aesthetic sensibilities in the school buildings Youji no Shiro had created. I personally think it is difficult to teach children about the arts. The key is exposing them to as much art as possible in their early childhood. So, I figured that the school buildings where children spend a lot of their time needed to be tasteful and creative. I consulted with Youji no Shiro before I retired from baseball, long before I decided on the location [of the school]—even before I thought about starting a nursery or kindergarten!

Q   **Could you tell us about the architectural designs of KR Kindergarten and Nursery and KS Primary School?**

A   KR Kindergarten and Nursery sits on a slope, which translates into tiered floors indoor. When I was looking for locations to build the school, I fell in love with this site. It is surrounded by the woods. I was, however, concerned that all the vegetation might get in the way. Thankfully, Youji no Shiro took full advantage of the environment in their design: they didn't cut down any trees and did their best to leave the site intact.

Hokkaido generally evokes an image of bountiful nature, but the winters are cold, and children spend a lot of time on their phones or playing video games. As a result, the region faces the challenges of childhood obesity and poor athletic ability. Our building gets kids moving and exercising quite naturally—this is another aspect I like about our building.

KS Primary School was renovated from an existing elementary school. Reusing existing structures aligns with the [United Nations] Sustainable Development Goals. I hope that the rough-hewn concrete surfaces exposed in the finished design would prompt children to cherish the old, as well as cultivate an awareness of sustainability.

〉
Night view of KS Primary
School

Q How do parents react to the spaces?

A Everyone is satisfied when I give a proper explanation about why the schools are built this way. I feel that they don't have a problem once they understand the logic that connects the design with our educational aspirations.

>
Science room of KS Primary
School

<
A corridor in KS Primary
School

Q What's your favorite spot in the KR Kindergarten and Nursery building?

A Beside the windows on the third floor; I love the view of the entire facility. Creating a "perfectly safe" school where no child even gets hurt probably translates into something flat and boring. A boldly designed nursery, like ours, is far more effective in stirring up kids' curiosity. Of course, we always take the essential precautions. Also, children get used to the space before you know it. Nursery owners need to truly believe in children's ability to adapt.

Q   You pivoted to education from a completely different industry. Given your unique position, could you share your thoughts on education today?

A   Our desire to create a new school that benefits from the fact that I was a complete outsider to the field of education. Don't get me wrong, our teachers and staff are all excellent and bring many years of school experience, but that same experience can sometimes turn into a bias. So, discussions with people like me, who challenge conventional wisdom, can produce new ways of doing things, while firmly respecting the values that both sides can yield. I hope our school continues to retain these distinctive characteristics.

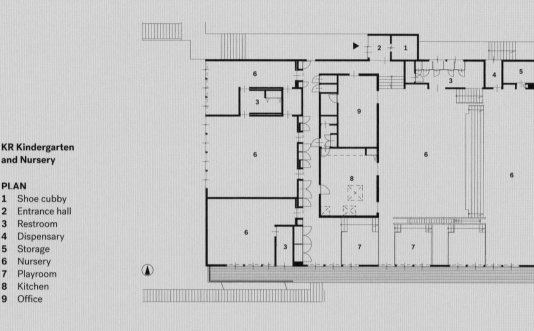

KR Kindergarten and Nursery

PLAN
1   Shoe cubby
2   Entrance hall
3   Restroom
4   Dispensary
5   Storage
6   Nursery
7   Playroom
8   Kitchen
9   Office

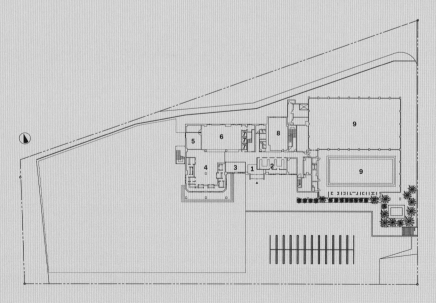

KS Primary School

PLAN
1   Entrance hall
2   Shoe cubby
3   Meeting room
4   Library
5   Principal's office
6   Office
7   Counseling room
8   Music room
9   Gymnasium

SLF Primary and Secondary School

Shenzhen, China

Infusing large-scale schools with natural environments

SLF Primary and Secondary School is a newly established elementary and junior high school in Shenzhen, China, for children aged 7 to 15 years old. The school's concept, "School of the Future," envisions an education space that empowers children to create their future with civility and grace.

Contemplation of the future must be done in consideration of our present-day environment. In a region where outdoor play is stifled by air pollution, it felt apropos to focus on conservation in the design of the new school building. The site was once a mountainside and still retains remnants of its rich natural surroundings. Rather than destroying it, our building fuses with the land to carry on its natural history. The towering rooftops, angled walls, and greenery planted on-site, along with other architectural components, harmonize with the surroundings and reduce the building's environmental burden. Our design also effectively utilizes natural sources of energy through—for example, channels for cross-ventilation, as well as filtering in natural daylight from the south-facing side to minimize the overreliance on mechanical equipment.

SLF Primary and Secondary School's simple design tones are a far cry from the arcane (in a sense of being an old-fashioned impression of) imagery the word "futuristic" can sometimes evoke. Here, people—the children, staff, parents—occupy center stage and form a vivid and radiant community. The open and transparent architecture facilitates children's relationship with their surroundings, as well as creates awareness within the community about the school's lively activities.

┐
Exterior view—the building seems to join with the hill in the background

>
School yard (rendering image)

COMPLETION: September 2021
AREA: 45,208 ft² (42,000 m²)
PHOTOGRAPHY: Raykwok

Liu Rongqing
Principal, SLF Primary and Secondary School

" Sensory enrichment and exposure to nature will undoubtedly be driving forces in creating the future. "

Q   **Could you give us an overview of SLF Primary and Secondary School?**
A   When we first began operations in September 2021, SLF Primary and Secondary School had about 400 students. Today, we are a combined elementary and junior high school with more than 1,000 students across nine grades: seven classes in elementary and two classes in junior high.

Q   **Why did you choose to entrust Youji no Shiro with the design of the new school building?**
A   Traditional schools value teaching and lesson-based learning. However, SLF is fundamentally different. For one, we emphasize autonomous learning. We aspire for the school's architecture to support our mission.

Youji no Shiro won the bid as our designer. They proposed that "creating the future" requires nurturing children's potential by exposing them to nature. Their vision perfectly aligned with the school's aim. We got to witness their commitment first hand as they worked hard on the project, and they also shared their input on everything, from design to management.

Q   **What aspects of the school's architecture do you find appealing?**
A   One of the building's most striking and unique features are the glass walls and surfaces. You get to see the school in its entirety, and where the children spend their time and so on. Such an open environment also allows plenty of natural light, which positively influences one's mental well-being. These features assure parents of their children's safety and helps maintain smooth communication among the children, parents, and teachers.

The design also takes cognizance of the school's surroundings. The building offers spaces where you can connect with the water and hills, against which the school is set. It's truly delightful to have such an environment as a place of learning.

Q   **What are the reactions of your students, their parents, and other stakeholders?**
A   When the school first opened, we even received compliments from the staff at the Shenzhen city office: "The school 'brims with *yang* [energy]." Parents and observers visiting the school would mention that the school "goes above and beyond conventional frameworks." At the risk of sounding repetitive, our priority is to ensure every child grows up and develops an authentic sense of self. We will continue to explore ways to promote children's individuality through education.

∧
Plant boxes and greenery incorporated along the boundary of each floor makes the terraced building look like a small hill (rendering image)

⟩
Classrooms are connected to the surrounding nature

PLAN

1 Overpass entrance
2 Sunken theater
3 Outdoor playground
4 Classroom
5 Office
6 Physics laboratory
7 Restroom
8 General rest area
9 Planting terrace
10 Planting area

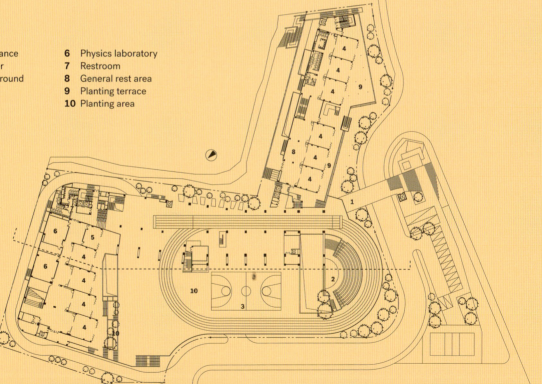

3

Key Designing Elements for Children's Spaces

AN Kindergarten, Kanagawa, Japan, Photo by
Kenjiro Yoshimi / studio BAUHAUS

Questioning
Conventional
Wisdom
to
Envision
Fun
and
Innovative
Spaces

Youji no Shiro's architectural designs for children inherently differ in tones, textures, materials, and design elements, but project a consistent underlying philosophy: we strive to create spaces that support the healthy growth and development of children.

This chapter discusses the elements that form our architectural designs, as well as the theories we draw on to envision a space.

Spaces with blind spots, or restrooms with large windows may be considered unconventional, but the purpose of these design features is to ensure that children enjoy their space. Though restrooms without windows allow privacy, and flat spaces enable parents and guardians to keep an eye on children, these features are often designed from an adult perspective.

Youji no Shiro's designs promote freedom of movement and challenge hidebound mindsets.

FM Nursery, Saitama, Japan, Photo by Ryuji Inoue

Playgrounds and Play Equipment

Integrate play areas with the preschool architecture

SP Nursery, Fukushima,
Japan

MRN Kindergarten and Nursery, Miyazaki, Japan

In preschools, playgrounds and playing equipment are critical for children to learn though play. However, designers continue to view playgrounds and playing equipment as separate aspects from the overall design, often leading to flat sites with token greenery and playground equipment inserted without much thought, merely for the sake of including these elements in the design.

Preschool reconstruction projects offer great opportunities for a variety of design creations, such as miniature hills made from surplus construction soil, or earthen tunnels for children to crawl through. Even dead spaces under stairs or pilotis can be turned into dens. Recognizing playgrounds as an integral part of preschool architecture opens up a range of creative possibilities, both on the playground and inside the building.

HN Nursery, Kanagawa, Japan

AM Kindergarten and Nursery, Kagoshima, Japan

KFB Kindergarten and Nursery, Kagoshima, Japan

HZ Kindergarten and
Nursery, Okinawa, Japan

AKK Nursery, Tokyo, Japan

DS Nursery, Ibaraki, Japan

Restrooms

Make restrooms bright and fun

YM Nursery, Tottori, Japan

Restrooms in Japan are usually located to the north of a building where less sunlight filters in, on the belief that they are dirty places that need to be hidden. Contemporary preschool architecture favors bright and clean restrooms. Youji no Shiro goes a step further to prioritize natural lighting over artificial illumination. This has a dual advantage—it benefits aesthetics and also the children's well-being.

It is also important to keep restroom floors dry, given that bacteria thrive on floors that are wet, even after they have been cleaned. Having natural sunlight flood restrooms helps keeps restroom floors dry, while also having a slight bactericidal effect. Overall, it helps maintain clean and bright restrooms.

We usually opt for bright and uplifting color palettes in the restrooms, and openings are carefully incorporated for natural ventilation. As children are highly responsive to fun elements and visual stimuli, they tend to visit the restrooms with no reservations.

KO Kindergarten, Ehime, Japan

KM Kindergarten and Nursery, Osaka, Japan

D1 Kindergarten and Nursery, Kumamoto, Japan

DS Nursery, Ibaraki, Japan

Dining Rooms

Spark interest through lunchrooms and views of the kitchen

SGC Nursery, Tokyo, Japan

Kitchens have long been relegated to basements or locations away from building entrances. Considering the importance of food and dietary education, Youji no Shiro proposes kitchen placements that are open and visible to children; we design lunchrooms as places where children can gather for meals. An open kitchen allows scrumptious aromas to travel through the compound, which spark children's curiosity in food preparation. Open, visible kitchens also allow children to see how their meals are prepared, which is similar to them watching their parents make dinner at home. This adds to their dietary education and creates opportunities to strike up conversations with the staff who prepare their meals. Youji no Shiro goes goes a step beyond to also engage in discussions with preschools to create spaces that align with their food policies and processes.

SK Nursery, Tokyo, Japan

ST Nursery, Saitama, Japan

TY Nursery, Mie, Japan

SM Nursery, Kanagawa, Japan

D1 Kindergarten and
Nursery, Kumamoto, Japan

Dens and Huts

Design small spaces that are meant for children only

FM Nursery, Saitama, Japan

Dens are often designed into the plan and placed either above or below staircases. Hut-like enclosures are another favorite and also often make their way into the design. These fun structures usually have narrow entrances—through which only children can pass—and small interiors, making them dedicated spaces for children, accessible only by them.

Understandably, some schools may prefer not to have "blind spots" such as these, but the benefits do outweigh the risk as areas like dens and forts support children's mental and emotional stability. It also allows them quiet time and a break from the noise and bustle. Not to mention, playing in secret forts is always exciting and fun!

Ouchi, Saga, Japan

M, N Nursery, Kanagawa, Japan

NFB Kindergarten and Nursery, Nara, Japan

Exercise

Create spaces that increase opportunities for exercise

OB Kindergarten and Nursery, Nagasaki, Japan

Modern lifestyles have resulted in decreased levels of physical activity among children, much to their detriment. Sadly, this seems to be a trend more commonly observed in developed countries. In Japan, the declining physical activity and stamina of children, in both urban areas and the suburbs, have gotten much media attention. Simply instructing children to exercise more is ineffective.

Youji no Shiro's architectural designs address this issue by incorporating bouldering walls in dead spaces under staircases, or connecting floors with playground equipment and designing wide corridors that allow children to almost run the perimeter of the school. These design aspects expand the range of physical activities that children can engage in, while also create distances that are conducive for them to run and play freely. This creative integration of play areas helps increase the children's level of physical activity through fun and exciting methods without having to actually change the size of the structure.

KO Kindergarten, Ehime, Japan

HZ Kindergarten and Nursery, Okinawa, Japan

Security

"Closed" does not guarantee security

ATM Nursery, Osaka, Japan

Needing to protect children from crimes and other lurking dangers is not a new idea and, in fact, very normal all over the world. However, is a tall fence around a preschool a foolproof approach to security?

The community can often play an important role in protecting children, too. A layout open to the neighborhood allows both the preschool staff and community members to watch over the children, while also ensuring that the preschool is not an isolated entity, but part of the townscape. Withstanding the surroundings, leaving a site sufficiently open can, on the contrary, enhance safety and security.

AKK Nursery, Tokyo, Japan

Materials

Keep it simple by retaining original materials, colors, and textures

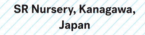
SR Nursery, Kanagawa, Japan

ibg School, Beijing, China

KM Kindergarten and Nursery, Osaka, Japan

Kinari Kindergarten and
Nursery, Shizuoka, Japan

WZY Kindergarten,
Guiyang, China

Many kindergartens and nurseries often use an extensive selection of primary colors to brighten up the spaces within. However, some of them sometimes miss the mark and unfortunately result looking like amusement parks rather than educational facilities. Keeping the use of colors to a minimum is a far better option, together with retaining the natural colors and appearance of the materials used, such as wood and iron.

This is Youji no Shiro's preferred approach, as an uncomplicated color palette and natural accents will aid the children's sensory development. Keeping the canvas simple gives children the opportunity to be more keenly aware of colors, so that they can easily familiarize themselves with them to identify colors they like. It also helps them develop a relation with colors, so that they can learn how to use them.

A selective use of colors ensures the space is not drowned out and has room to unfold and reveal itself. After all, children themselves should be the creators of the most vivid colors in a space.

Diversities

Adopt diversity as a starting point for design

Youji no Shiro regards disabilities as a manifestation of individuality, rather than a handicap. Irrespective of their disability—whether physical or mental—children who have special needs often go through a different range of experiences. Therefore, it is important to not focus on impairments and instead adopt diversity as a starting point for design. Every child's abilities, strengths, and weaknesses differ, and the adults around them play a crucial role in helping them recognize their individualism.

Designs tailored for special needs children include multisensory environments, such as a Snoezelen room, to help reduce feelings of anxiety and lessen stress levels. Materials for both the inside and outside of these preschools are also carefully selected, with the preference being natural materials that are gentle to touch and which have pleasing scents.

KH Center, Tokyo, Japan

LSC Center, Nagasaki, Japan

LSF Center, Nagasaki, Japan

Rooms for Infants

Create a space where the babies and toddlers instinctively feel comfortable

KNO Nursery, Nagasaki, Japan

HN Nursery, Kanagawa, Japan

Design thinking generally differs when creating spaces for infants. Unlike older children, babies spend most of their time in a sleeping position. Based on this, it is important to consider ceiling design and lighting thoroughly and carefully.

Inviting natural light into a room and the use of artificial lighting are also key points that are deliberated on. The type of flooring is also an important aspect, especially when considered in tandem with babies' developmental milestones, such as crawling. To that extent, coarse or overly textured flooring is usually rejected as it will cause an infant's sensitive skin discomfort when they crawl over it. Level variations can be incorporated, however, as such design features will benefit the growing infant. The floors need not be flat and can have small rises to help develop infants' physical strength. Using natural materials along with incorporating nature, such as trees and lawns, also promote physical and mental well-being.

Locality

Design based on the study of the history and culture of the site

L ocality is a foremost consideration in the design process. Given the homogenizing effect of modernization, fewer children are aware of their town's history and culture. Kindergartens and nurseries should offer children the opportunity to learn about their local area, so that they can grow to appreciate it. During the conceptualizing stage in a project, the natural features and unique form of the site and surroundings are closely studied to ensure that the design aligns with the location.

YM Nursery, Tottori, Japan

AKK Nursery, Tokyo, Japan

M, N Nursery, Kanagawa, Japan

Sustainability

Prioritize an ecology that matches preschools and their landscapes

OA Kinergarten, Saitama, Japan

CLC Beijing, Beijing, China

HZ Kindergarten and
Nursery, Okinawa, Japan

AK Nursery, Ibaraki, Japan

Childcare facilities play a key role in nurturing children to become responsible global citizens, which means also being conscious of the environment they inhabit and its ecological issues.

To create this awareness and incorporate sustainable features that uphold our "environment conscious" message, Youji no Shiro integrates solar-powered systems and other similar equipment in many preschool designs.

An environmental perspective has become indispensable in present-day architecture and and we consider a variety of solutions to enable this, which include cross-ventilation to reduce the use of electricity and gas and wooden constructions to curb carbon dioxide emissions. Construction methods that do not rely heavily on equipment are also meticulously explored.

As Japan stretches far, from north to south, creating climatic conditions that differ considerably among the regions, our designs call for different approaches, depending on the location of the preschool, to ensure that the design fits the climate of the site and the form of the building.

Chapter

4

Furniture for Children

A family using the 'Ladder Chair', Photo by Kosuke Tamura

Designing
the
Components
and
Details
Within
the
Space

As an architectural design team, Youji no Shiro has long struggled with the confliction that we cannot design every single detail within the space, particularly furniture, logo, uniform, and other similar accessories and identifying elements that complete the space. Such details play as significant a role as the building and space themselves. To overcome this restriction, the company KIDS DESIGN LABO (KDL) was established, making up a professional creative team that focuses on designing the various items—other than architecture—that fill children's facilities.

Items made for children are often either designed with popular cartoon characters, or dismayingly, contain collisions of too many bright colors in a single item.

While colors and popular characters are attractive and engaging to children, such "camouflage" also risks diminishing their appreciation for genuine things. The things that children see, touch, smell, use, and experience in the early stages of their development go toward shaping their perspectives, mindset, and outlook in their later years. Hence items/toys that they are exposed to, and which form their "circle" in their early years, need to be very well designed and nurturing.

This chapter highlights targeted furniture designs created by KDL, which are sometimes incorporated into Youji no Shiro's preschool projects.

Round Chair

(9 colors)
Ash

S	M	L	XL
Ø320 mm × H280 mm	Ø350 mm × H280 mm	Ø370 mm × H280 mm	Ø370 mm × H400 mm

A simple round stool with four legs. With nothing to lean on, children are naturally guided to sit straight. The XL size is suitable for an adult to use.

All sizes of the chair can be used as a small side table that can be effortlessly coordinated to fit any décor.

Chairs come in four sizes, children can choose a size suited to their height. Stacking is also possible

Solo Sofa

Wood: 1 color / Leather: 6 varieties
Frame (ash); Leather (sheep, cow, goat, pig, horse, deer); Cushion (urethane foam)

W469 mm × D460 mm × H400 mm / SH300 mm

Just like adults, children also want to have that perfect couch for reading their favorite picture books. This genuine leather sofa with comfortable, soft cushions makes them feel as "cool" as the grown-ups surrounding them.

The seat of the sofa is made of genuine leather; children can observe the aging process of the leather. The finish brings out the color of the leather itself

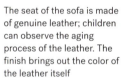

Sit-back Chair

(9 colors)
Ash

S	**M**	**L**
W380 mm × D401 mm × H390 mm	W380 mm × D412 mm × H410 mm	W380 mm × D430 mm × H440 mm
SH240 mm	SH260 mm	SH290 mm

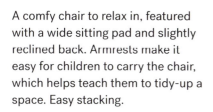

A comfy chair to relax in, featured with a wide sitting pad and slightly reclined back. Armrests make it easy for children to carry the chair, which helps teach them to tidy-up a space. Easy stacking.

When children sit with their hands resting on the arms or seat of the chair, they naturally straighten their backs

Square Chair

(9 colors)
Ash

Bronze, Decorative Items and Homeware Design Award, A'Design Award 2019

XS	**S**	**M**	**L**
W245 mm × D250 mm × H340 mm	W300 mm × D270 mm × H400 mm	W310 mm × D290 mm × H440 mm	W340 mm × D320 mm × H490 mm
SH200 mm	SH240 mm	SH260 mm	SH290 mm

A simple square chair with minimal embellishments; fits in all interior styles. The frame/backrest makes the chair easily movable, even by small children. All the sizes are stackable.

The colored versions are finished with naturally derived paints. The light color blends in with any interior

Square Armed Chair

(9 colors)
Ash

XXS
W245 mm × D250 mm × H300 mm / SH160 mm

XS
W245 mm × D250 mm × H340 mm / SH200 mm

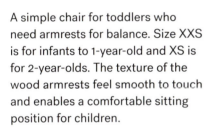

A simple chair for toddlers who need armrests for balance. Size XXS is for infants to 1-year-old and XS is for 2-year-olds. The texture of the wood armrests feel smooth to touch and enables a comfortable sitting position for children.

A carefully crafted chair with no nails or screws showing on the surface

Ladder Chair

(9 colors)
Ash

Iron, Decorative Items and Homeware Design Award, A'Design Award 2019

Upcoming product
Details subject to change due to continual improvements

A chair that keeps up with growing children. The height of the seat and footrest can be adjusted as children grow to ensure a comfortable sitting posture. It fits with a variety of table designs and can also be used by adults without the footrest.

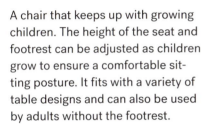

All KDL furniture is made of natural wood and is very easy to maintain

TABLE

Round Table

(9 colors)
Ash

S	M	L
Ø1,190 mm × H500 mm	Ø1,240 mm × H500 mm	Ø1,290 mm × H500 mm

With its circular tabletop, it seems like the Round Table was tailored just to match our Round Chair. Because the legs are fitted at the center of the base, it can be easily used from all directions. The table can also be color coordinated with our Square Chair to match. Stackable when needed.

The Round Table can seat many

Square Table

(9 colors)
Ash (with steel corner brackets)

S	**M**	**L**
W880 mm × D450 mm × H430 mm	W970 mm × D450 mm × H460 mm	W1,060 mm × D450 mm × H520 mm

A simple four-legged table that pairs seamlessly with our Square Chair. Foldable legs make the table easy to stack. It's a perfect work desk for children and also makes an ideal side table for adults.

This chic table is designed to blend with any home interior

Custom-built Furniture

KIDS DESIGN LABO (KDL) also offers custom-made furniture
to suit a variety of preschool spaces and client requests.

HN Nursery, Kanagawa, Japan

This furniture for toddlers serves a dual function as a table and a chair.

YM Nursery, Tottori, Japan

Far right: a bench made by stacking scraps of local lumber. Right: a bed for infants. Bottom left: colorful stools for staff and guests.

KB Primary and Secondary School, Nagasaki, Japan

Top left: built-in storage shelves. Lower left: desks and chairs for students designed to age and enhance the character of the wood. Right: indoor playground equipment made of solid wood in the shape of a house.

D1 Kindergarten and Nursery, Kumamoto, Japan

Luggage storage units tailored for the school. Each child uses his/her assigned storage cubby while at school to help establish ownership and responsibility over his/her belongings.

5

Visual

Identity

KB Primary and Secondary School, Nagasaki, Japan, Photo by Kosuke Tamura

Ways
to
Establish
Brand
Image
in
Children's
Facilities

I t is difficult for any kindergarten or nursery to stay in a leading position, especially against the backdrop of a falling birth rate. To continuously enjoy the privilege, benefit, and success of having attained a leading position, and maintain a lead establishing the brand with clear definitions is key.

Aware of the impact a brand's visual identity (VI) can have on people, as well as the association it can create with the brand and the ripple effects it can lead to—such as "top-of-mind recall"—Youji no Shiro and KIDS DESIGN LABO provide consultation services for VI design. In the context of preschool, nurseries, and kindergartens, VI elements include the school logo, uniform, and other brand/school accessories, such as signage, stationery, school-produced literature, and even school events. The following are some samples of VI design specifically crafted by Youji no Shiro and KIDS DESIGN LABO, sometimes in collaboration with other designers.

HZ Kindergarten and Nursery, Okinawa, Japan, Photo by Toru Kometani

UNIFORMS

Uniforms help create a distinctive attachment between children (students) and their schools. They also create awareness about the school among the residents, making them more vigilant about keeping an eye on the children and watching over them, in turn bonding the community and establishing a strong and cohesive unit made up of teachers, parents, caregivers, and members of the community.

DRM Preschool

The uniforms for DRM preschool were designed in collaboration with the children's wear brand Kitutuki. A base tone of deep blue is selected to reflect the abundant water resources in the area where the school is located.

HZ Kindergarten and Nursery

The school building is located in semi-tropical Okinawa. To match, the school's uniform includes T-shirts printed with the school logo accompanied by different flower motifs—such as a chrysanthemum or tulip—that identify the wearer with a specific class according to the flower.

KB Primary and Secondary School

This uniform was designed in collaboration with FUJITO, a popular clothing brand. As the school is located in a port town where the U.S. Navy has a base and the town has a history of diverse cultures, the uniform sports the international Ivy League ensemble with eye-catching plaid bottoms and blazers.

UNIFORMS

ibg School

Their overalls-style uniform in denim is highly durable and also comfortable for the children's daily wear. The fabric attains a unique character with use, as is the nature of denim, making the uniform almost personalized to each child.

OA Kindergarten

OA Kindergarten's uniform is a polo shirt with a logo sewn on the back and a design on the sleeves. The uniform displays a monotone color scheme to match the minimalist, modern-style preschool.

LOGO

A logo is an integral part of an organization's identity. The preschool's logo features on the building, business card, stationery, and uniforms, making it an element of brand identity that extends beyond the school's premises. This makes it important for the logo to align with the vision of the preschool. Logos are often designed in collaboration with external graphic designers.

MATSUGASAKINOMORI
KINDERGARTEN

MM Kindergarten

The logo, consisting of hand-drawn triangles, was designed in collaboration with designer Chikako Oguma. The growing series of triangles represents children growing up in a new environment.

IINO OYAKO NURSERY

IO Nursery

A collaboration project with designer Chikako Oguma, the logo is made up of different shapes in different sizes, indicating the nursery's philosophy, which is to value each child's diversity and uniqueness.

ST Nursery

This collaboration with designer Chikako Oguma designs a logo for this school with swan icons that appear like children drawings, along with the preschool's name. The logo's coral-blue color represents the river in the town where the preschool is located.

OA Kindergarten

The logo is a graphical representation of the preschool's initials, "O" and "A." Graphical interpretations of a circular and triangular building block—learning toys often used in preschools—denote the letters so that children can draw a link in the similarities between the toy they know so well and the logo, and thus better relate to the logo design.

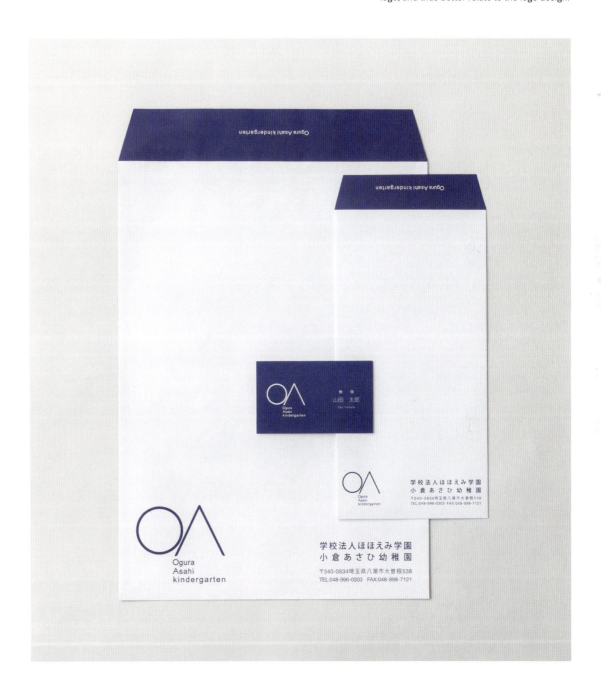

SIGNAGE

Signs are usually used to indicate the names of rooms within the school building. Steering away from standard, conventional designs, the signage design opted for in these projects are based on the characteristics of the building and created to be attractive and eye-catching.

HZ Kindergarten and Nursery

The signs are designed as the flowers after which each class is named.

AN Kindergarten

The signs are designed as houses of different shapes.

DS Nursery

The characters on the signs appear like they are being blown away by the wind to match the concept used in the preschool building.

SIGNAGE

OA Kindergarten

The signs represent the characteristics of the preschool building and are made of wood with a black steel frame.

OB Kindergarten and Nursery

The signs display the nature motifs associated with the class name.

EVENTS AND WORKSHOPS

When designing a space, it is important to consider features that will create excitement and enthusiasm within the children, and which will also reflect the preschool's identity. Youji no Shiro's design work is not limited to just architecture and space, often going beyond the two to include other elements that serve to tailor the school's unique identity. These elements span a range of special events and workshops on selected topics (such as food education) conducted by instructors who have been invited to the school. They also include designing venues within the preschool compound that are tailored to promote open communication and interactions.

Kitutuki Workshop

The Kitutuki Workshop was conducted by a group of designers that worked on textiles and other similar media. Children and adults used printing blocks and paints to create delightful patterns on aprons for children. The workshop was positively received and participants put their craft skills to work with much enthusiasm. It concluded with a fashion parade to showcase the aprons.

Food Education Workshop

Food researchers were invited to the school to conduct a workshop on food education. Informational presentations were paired with engaging activities and the children also enjoyed making hand-rolled sushi using ingredients sourced from local stores. Through this workshop, the children learnt the importance and value of fresh, locally produced food; they were very happy with their meals and even asked for seconds.

WORKSHOPS

Photo by Yoichi Onoda

Where Good Designs and Brand-new Values are Generated

A typical morning at Youji no Shiro starts with staff reporting for work at 8 am, with some of them randomly trickling into a café next to the office to enjoy some breakfast and catch up with colleagues on the projects on hand and tasks for the day that need to be completed. Our routines and discussions may have changed since our parent company, Hibino Sekkei, was established in 1972, but our end goal to add value to a client's business through thoughtfully designed architecture still remains the crux of our projects.

Hibino Sekkei began the business by focusing on architectural design that spanned a range of project categories, but in 2001 they streamlined their design unit to be more specialized in selected categories. That has proven to be the right move for the organization as a whole, and we are very thankful for the opportunities we have been given to design facilities for young children in various countries as Youji no Shiro; "Youji no Shiro" translates to "Castle for Young Children."

Both of Youji no Shiro's offices are located in Atsugi City, Kanagawa Prefecture, Japan, and are certain to surprise anyone who visits, appearing very different from typical architectural design firms. The fact that we have chosen to locate our base in Kanagawa Prefecture, next to Tokyo, and not Tokyo itself—as many major firms do—differentiates us even further within this service tier. Even as our business grew, we chose to remain in this "bedroom town" of Tokyo instead of relocating to Tokyo for we wholeheartedly appreciated Atsugi's strong urban aspects: it has good access to airports, has big towns that are well-known, even abroad—like Shinjuku and Shibuya— and of course we can't leave out its railway station vicinity, which you can use to get whatever you need. Atsugi's suburban areas are also home to many *onsen* (hot springs), and have beautiful, extending country views in which you can often spot wild animals. And so, we decided that we would rather enjoy such a splendid natural and inviting environment than endure the hassle of overcrowded Tokyo. The pleasing and relaxing environment is also more conducive to the creative aspects of our work, like space designing and proposals.

Atsugi is blessed with a rich, natural environment that you would never get, let alone ask for, in Tokyo. These natural surroundings have created a great selection of local producers and farmers who are full of curiosity, who put their heart in their work and their fresh produce—we know because we have actually met with them and tasted their freshly grown ingredients. These delicious,

locally sourced ingredients are the backbone of Restaurant 2343, a restaurant on the upper floor of our main office, and FOOD LABO 2343, a deli café in our other office near Hon-Atsugi Station. (So, now it's understandable why staff get together for breakfast.) Not only are these food venues frequented by staff, they are also a novel way to make an impression on clients and introduce our versatility when we host them in these restaurants for project discussions.

Also, since food and the right diet are one of the essential elements in facilities catered for young children, we thought it would be good for us to get some education and experience on the subject, as well as deepen our knowledge, which will be beneficial when designing eating spaces at kindergartens and nurseries. A home-grown venue where we could test/realize the best diet for both ourselves and the children we would serve presented as an ideal solution, and so an F&B portfolio was accordingly included in our service line-up in 2017.

As the café and restaurant ventures show, Youji no Shiro strives to redefine *and refine* our knowledge and experience by making an effort to learn in-depth about the different fields we choose to explore, and by drawing links to our existing designing services so that we may extend our service fields.

Aligned with such efforts was the launch of KIDS DESIGN LABO (KDL) in 2016, under which we design children's furniture, uniforms, school signages, and even logos for kindergartens and nurseries. Through our many projects over the years designing spaces for children, we were often frustrated with not being able to control ancillary issues like how these spaces would be used after completion, the type of furniture that would fill the area, and even what signage designs the kindergartens would select, and whether it would complement and appropriately convey the essence of our design and the spirit of the school. To elaborate: for example, plastic furniture would be totally unacceptable and inappropriate for a space designed around natural materials, and childish signage would be a frightful mismatch with a chic space. No matter how well, or how beautifully and creatively a space has been designed, without the correct accessories and accents—such as interior furnishings and signage—the design will fall short, playing out instead as non-cohesive and "off." It would be hard to create an attractive nursery or kindergarten without thinking about the space in totality, which includes essentially every related element. A holistic design aids in improving the quality of the space, and thereby the quality of the education.

Establishing KDL has definitely been a step in the right direction and it has allowed us to specifically tailor and better attune the end result. KDL have been involved on many projects with Youji no Shiro as the division considering the overall branding of the school, while Youji no Shiro focuses on design. There are also many other times when KDL operates on its own momentum, engaging in projects individually, as a unit different from Youji no Shiro.

In 2020, we expanded our service range yet again with KIDS SMILE LABO (KSL) to focus on the administrative and professional facets of facilities for children. KIDS SMILE LABO offers consulting services for kindergartens and nurseries in areas that include the

designing of educational policies for newly established kindergarten facilities, staff training, and teaching materials, among others. We have been successful in this venture, even receiving project proposals from outside Japan.

In this book, we introduce the architectural and designing works by Youji no Shiro design and KIDS DESIGN LABO. Some of the kindergarten facilities designed by us have received much praise with world-class awards, and some are very highly talked about in Japan. We have been interviewed many times on our work, and are sometimes asked, "How are you able to design an attractive kindergarten facility like this?" It's a compliment we appreciate; we are very thankful to receive such validating moments of recognition.

We produced this book to share our design concepts in the hope that they inspire the reader in crafting their own unique designs for children's facilities. We think of a space as being more than a space. We value all the "contents" in the container called space as significant as the container itself. There are still many great and wonderful designs waiting to be created, and many new ventures waiting to become adventures.

You never know, you may find yourself reading a Hibino Sekkei picture book as a bedtime story to your child one night, or your toddler's next favorite toy, taken everywhere with him or her, could be one of our toys.

We will continue making the lives of children and the adults around them more enjoyable through what we produce, because is what makes us happy.

About the Author

Photo by Kenichi Yamaguchi

Taku Hibino

Founder, CEO, and Chairman
Hibino Sekkei Youji no Shiro

Born in 1972 in Kanagawa Prefecture, Japan, Hibino graduated from Koga-kuin University in Tokyo. In 1991 he founded Youji no Shiro within Hibino Sekkei, a brand dedicated to the design of children's facilities. In 2016, Hibino founded KIDS DESIGN LABO Inc., a designing and consultancy company.

A year later, he opened "2343," a restaurant with three other outlets in Kanagawa Prefecture. In 2018, he established a Chinese branch and in 2021, he founded KIDS SMILE LABO, the first nursery run by Hibino Sekkei.

Begun as an architectural company, Hibino Sekkei is successfully expanding its business portfolio. Taku Hibino is now the acting CEO and chairman of the company.

Business Field

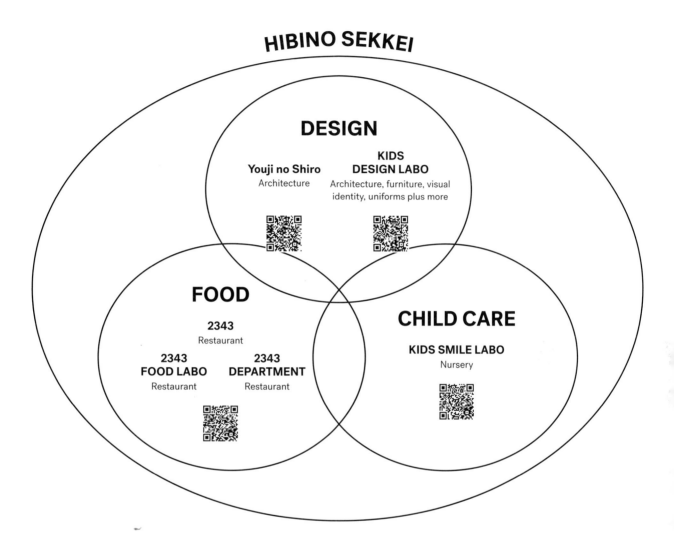

HIBINO SEKKEI

DESIGN

Youji no Shiro
Architecture

KIDS DESIGN LABO
Architecture, furniture, visual identity, uniforms plus more

FOOD

2343
Restaurant

2343 FOOD LABO
Restaurant

2343 DEPARTMENT
Restaurant

CHILD CARE

KIDS SMILE LABO
Nursery

About Youji no Shiro

Youji no Shiro is a design team that specializes in the architectural design of children's facilities such as nurseries, kindergartens, and preschools. As of 2022, Youji no Shiro has designed more than 540 children's spaces all over the world.

https://e-ensha.com

The World Designed for Children

Complete Works of Hibino Sekkei Youji no Shiro and KIDS DESIGN LABO

AUTHORS
Taku Hibino, Hibino Sekkei, Youji no Shiro

> **HIBINO SEKKEI**
> https://hibinosekkei.com

> **YOUJI NO SHIRO**
> https://e-ensha.com

> **KIDS DESIGN LABO**
> https://kidsdesignlabo.com

EDITORS
Sawako Akune / GINGRICH
Daisuke Saito / GINGRICH
Kentaro Wada / GINGRICH
Hiroki Suzukawa / GINGRICH

ART DIRECTOR / GRAPHIC DESIGNER
Kohei Sekida

PHOTOGRAPHERS
Toshinari Soga / studio BAUHAUS
Kenjiro Yoshimi / studio BAUHAUS
Ryuji Inoue
Kosuke Tamura
Yoichi Onoda
Toru Kometani
Hiromi Asai
Keisuke Fukamizu
Raykwok
Ivan Cho
Kenichi Yamaguchi

PROJECT COORDINATION
Yuma Masukawa / Hibino Sekkei

KFB Kindergarten and Nursery, Kagoshima, Japan, Photo by Ryuji Inoue

Published in Australia in 2023 by
The Images Publishing Group Pty Ltd
ABN 89 059 734 431

Offices

Melbourne
Waterman Business Centre
Suite 64, Level 2 UL40
1341 Dandenong Road
Chadstone, Victoria 3148
Australia
Tel: +61 3 8564 8122

New York
6 West 18th Street 4B
New York City, NY 10011
United States
Tel: +1 212 645 1111

Shanghai
6F, Building C,
838 Guangji Road
Hongkou District,
Shanghai 200434
China
Tel: +86 021 31260822

books@imagespublishing.com
www.imagespublishing.com

Copyright © The Images Publishing Group Pty Ltd 2023
The Images Publishing Group Reference Number: 1609

A catalogue record for this book is available from the National Library of Australia

Title: The World Designed for Children: Complete Works of Hibino Sekkei Youji no Shiro and KIDS DESIGN LABO
Authors: Taku Hibino, Hibino Sekkei Youji no Shiro
ISBN: 9781864708875

Printed by Toppan Excel (Dongguan) Printing CO.,LTD., China

IMAGES has included on its website a page for special notices in relation to this and its other publications. Please visit www.imagespublishing.com